LIVE | DEAD

The Story

28 DAYS OF LIVING THE BOOK OF ACTS
WITH IRANIAN BELIEVERS

shawn smucker

Published by Influence Resources
1445 N. Boonville Ave.
Springfield, Missouri 65802

Cover design and interior formatting by Prodigy Pixel.

Note: All of the names in this book, as well as some identifying details, have been changed to protect the anonymity of the storytellers and their families, many of whom remain in Iran and continue to share the gospel despite increasing threats, imprisonment, and even death.

ISBN: 978-1-62912-113-0
17 16 15 14 • 1 2 3 4 5

CONTENTS

Why Live Dead?

BY RAYMOND OLIVER

"When Christ calls a man, he bids him come and die."

DIETRICH BONHOEFFER

For Haik Hovsepian, Mehdi Dibaj, and several other Iranian church leaders, to live dead meant real martyrdom, death for the sake of the gospel. For Hossein Soodmand, to live dead meant following Christ to the Iranian gallows knowing that in doing so he left behind his blind wife to care for his children and their grief stricken congregation. (His body was thrown into the city dump by his executioners.)

But what does it mean for *us* to live dead? It certainly isn't helpful to suffer guilt when our life on earth continues while that of others has been cut short. We must, however, find the cross prepared for us. We must find the place to empty ourselves for Him. We must strive against the constant tide of selfishness and find Christ in death to self.

We are fond of Christ's words in John 10:10, "The thief comes only to steal and kill and destroy; I have come that they may have life, and have it to the full." It's easy to forget however, that the resurrected life follows, rather than precedes, the crucified life.

While the sacrifices made in order to live dead vary greatly from person to person, the reason to live dead remains constant. Death is Christ's call to us: "Then (Jesus) said to them all: 'Whoever wants to be my disciple must deny themselves and take up their cross daily and follow me.'" (Luke 9:23)

We live dead because it is the only way that those who are spiritually dead might be brought to life. If I were doing exactly as I wished right now, I wouldn't be living in a new and strange land. I wouldn't be learning a strange and difficult language. If I were doing exactly as I wished, I would be somewhere near the west coast of the United States and one of my grandchildren would be on my lap. But Jesus has called me elsewhere, and there are so many who haven't heard the gospel. So I choose to live dead, not grudgingly but in anticipation of resurrection. I carry, in my death, the love of God, who is unwilling that any should perish, to a people who have yet to hear—a people I'm growing to love—in a land that resists my entry: Iran!

Finding a Hidden Church

Three of us got off the train somewhere in Istanbul, Turkey, and walked into the dark, rainy night. We were looking for something few people in the world have ever seen: a church of Iranian people serving God in the Middle East. Cars passed by, their tires kicking up a cloudy mist behind them. We walked out of the small train station and headed west down the long, cracked sidewalk.

Istanbul is located in both Asia and Europe. On that night we walked through the European side. Minarets rose up in the distance, marking some of the largest mosques in the world. The old wall of Constantinople formed a flat, dark silhouette against the center of the city shining beyond.

We walked past a darkened playground. To our left, ferry boats lined the Sea of Marmara, the same water that flows south into the Aegean Sea, and then farther south into the Mediterranean. If you look at a modern map of Turkey, certain cities might catch your attention: Antioch, Rhodes, Ephesus. On the other side of the Aegean, in modern-day Greece, you might notice Thessalonica and Corinth.

The entire region is saturated with Christian history going back to the first days of the early church. Paul journeyed not once . . . not twice . . . but four times through modern-day Turkey, encouraging, challenging, and exhorting the world's first believers. I wondered if he had ever walked along the sea on a rainy night as I was doing. I wondered if he had ever crept through the darkness, looking for one man in particular who would lead him to a group of believers.

We turned a corner and approached a small bridge where the train raced overhead, shaking the ground, groaning and squealing against the rails. A man leaned against the arch, partially hidden in the shadows. We walked towards him.

"Hi, I'm Shawn," I said. He smiled and nodded.

"Follow me."

He led us down a few narrow alleys, past closed shops with quiet upstairs apartments. Cars were parked up on the curb, all facing one direction, so close together I wondered how any of them ever got out.

"They're not used to having visitors," the man explained to us. "They might be rather suspicious at first. Some of them have been arrested in Iran numerous times. Some of them still have family in Iran, so they might not be comfortable having their interview recorded. Or having their pictures taken."

I nodded, trying hard to keep up with the man as his stride quickened.

"We're running a little late," he said as he turned into a darkened storefront. We walked through the glass door, then through another door, then up a flight of stairs, around a corner, and through a final door.

There it was: an Iranian church in Istanbul, Turkey.

Fifteen or so people sat in a circle, singing in Persian. We pulled up chairs behind them and tried not to make a sound.

The room's light felt extra bright after our trek through the dark part of the city. Soon one of the men stood up and began to preach. The people in the folding chairs paged eagerly through their Bibles, hanging on to every word. Every so often, our guide leaned over and translated for us in whispered English.

After the service ended, everyone came over and welcomed us. They were kind, and the ones learning English were eager to practice their language skills with us. They gave us cups of strong, hot Turkish tea and told us that a few of the people wanted to share their stories with me. So we set up three chairs in the far corner, one for me, one for the person sharing their story, and one for the interpreter. I turned on my recorder.

There were heartbreaking stories of young men and women forsaken by their families after they left Islam. There were harsh stories of abuse and police brutality. But there was also an intense amount of hope. For even in the most remote parts of Iran, where no one has preached the gospel, where there is no voice showing them the Way, Jesus is still made known . . . in the dreams of the people living there, people who have never heard the name of Jesus.

There were stories of churches continuing on even after their pastors were killed. Stories of escape. Stories of those determined to return to Iran to share the good news.

During the next year, I spoke with Iranian Christians from around the world. I worshiped with a large group of them in Missouri, I spoke with an apartment of Iranian men and women in Los Angeles, and I Skyped with more Iranians in Istanbul whose families still lived in Iran.

Their stories were varied. Some of them were shunned by their families after converting, while others were not. Some fled from Iran after becoming Christians while others didn't come to faith until after they left. Some stayed in Iran for many years, spreading the gospel. Some told stories of an Iranian government that was mostly ambivalent about their church's existence, while others told of a government that employs any means to root out the church and destroy it. Some are afraid that if they return they will be arrested, while others visit on a fairly regular basis.

But, again, the constant thread through all of the stories was hope. Hope that their families would find the truth, just as they themselves had. Hope that the Holy Spirit would continue to lead them. Hope that Iran would turn as a nation and follow Christ.

These are their stories.

We feel it's important to note that while many of the stories in this book are told by those who have left Iran, this is only because we were unable to gather stories from inside Iran and not because the majority of Christians are leaving. There is a vibrant underground church in Iran.

Please join with us and pray "through" this book, that the church in Iran would continue to grow strong and that God would help you to understand how best to become involved with the effort there: through intercession, financial support, or by going.

HOW TO USE THIS BOOK

This book is designed to be a twenty-eight-day journey into the book of Acts during which you'll encounter true stories of Iranian Christians. Each day corresponds with a chapter in the book of Acts and includes a name and photo of an Iranian as well as a compelling, true story told by an Iranian Christian, along with a Live | Dead Challenge. There will be some space after each story for a written response as you consider that day's chapter from Acts and the Iranian you have met in the pages.

There are many ways to use this book, but we suggest the following:

- Read one chapter each day, followed by the corresponding chapter in Acts.
- Take each Live | Dead Challenge seriously.
- Pray for the person or people in each story, that God would continue to give them the strength and perseverance they need.
- Pray for the country of Iran, that the borders would open and that the hearts and minds of the people would become even more receptive to the gospel.
- Pray that Christians from around the world would feel a call to go to Iran and live out their faith in that country.
- Ask Jesus if He wants you to go—to live and work among the Iranian people.
- Record your thoughts, reflections, and prayers in the journal spaces provided or in your own journal if you need additional space to write.
- Work through the book with your family, coworkers, or a group of friends.
- Keep each other accountable to the Live | Dead Challenges.

Prepare to journey into the world of Iranian Christians, a world that closely resembles the early church in the book of Acts. Prepare to be changed.

egree but no jobs. I would like to marry and... Many of my peers use drugs to escape. ...at will happen to me if I change... ...of my family? I am afr... ...n fear. On the Internet... ...ommon. The love of Jesus... ...friends know... ...somet... ...somet... ...I feel sad. Sometimes I... ...the tr... was born... ...hope... Who can I talk to? I can never please... ...paradi... I live in...

DAY ONE

Ava

THE APPEARANCE

After [Jesus'] suffering, he presented himself to them and gave
many convincing proofs that he was alive. He appeared to them
over a period of forty days and spoke about the kingdom of God.

ACTS 1:3

Jesus came to me in a dream thirty years ago, when I was in my late twenties. In those days, I knew Jesus only as a name. I had never read the Scriptures, and I had no idea what Christianity was about. It was shortly after the Iranian Revolution, and I was a strict Muslim, seeking Allah with all my heart. I wanted to know Allah. I wanted to hear his voice. But praying to Allah made me feel like I was going around in circles, and my cries were met with silence.

Then one night I had a dream. I was running through the countryside, terrified because I wasn't wearing my *hijab*, the traditional Muslim covering that I never left home without. Men chased me, and I felt exposed, in danger. If they caught me, and

I wasn't covered, I knew they would beat me . . . or worse. It had been many years since I had been out in public without my hijab, and a sense of panic filled me.

I arrived at the edge of a beautiful garden filled with oak trees, the kind of trees I now see in California where I live. There were two lines of oaks, and I ran down the middle of them, looking over my shoulder, waiting for the men to catch up to me, to grab me.

Then I saw a man sitting on a limb in the last tree. I knew Him as soon as I saw Him, but at first I wasn't sure of His name. It was like seeing someone I had once known very long ago. Beneath where He sat, in the middle of the tree-lined lane, was a metal door, standing there by itself. I walked up to the door and stared at it. Then I knocked. The metal door felt hard and cold on my knuckles.

"God, who are you?" I cried out. "Where are you?"

As soon as I shouted those things, I heard a voice. It was the man sitting on the tree branch. He had a beautiful, gentle voice. I had never heard a sound like it before in my life. I have never heard anything like it since.

"Why are you crying, Ava?" He asked me. "Why are you so upset and worried?"

Up until that point, I had an idea who this man was, but when He spoke, I knew for certain. His beautiful eyes were like a magnet, and they sent power through me, like an electric shock. It wasn't painful; it was invigorating.

"Do you know My name?" He said, "I will protect you. I will cover you."

"Are you Jesus Christ?" I asked.

He smiled.

"Now you know My name. I will protect you and save you. I will cover you."

Somehow, He reached down and grabbed me and set me next to Him on the branch. All fear left me. I knew I was safe. His eyes were beautiful, and I will never forget His face, His smile, and the way He spoke.

"I will protect you for the rest of your life," He said. "But first, I want to show you something."

He opened his hand and there it was . . . a large cross.

"I know," I said, remembering things I didn't know I had forgotten. "That is the one they crucified you on."

"This is for you, Ava," He said, smiling such a kind smile. "You are going to be protected and saved by Me for the rest of your life."

Then I woke up.

I started to weep, not because I was sad but because I was overwhelmed by the reality of the dream. Why did Jesus come to me in a dream? How did I know who He was? How did I know His name was Jesus?

I had a friend I thought might be a Christian, although we never talked about her faith. It was too dangerous for her to be open about it, especially in those early days after the Revolution. I called her right away and told her about my dream.

"What does this mean?" I asked her, desperate for answers.

She sighed.

"I don't know what it means, Ava, but so many of us long to see Him like that. To see His face the way you did. To hear His voice. I believe He has a plan for you."

After many years of seeking God, from that moment on I found Him. After I was baptized, it was like a puzzle came together. I realized that I wasn't here on earth for my own purpose but for the purposes of Jesus Christ. The day I realized this, the day I was baptized, was the happiest day of my life.

LIVE | DEAD CHALLENGE

When Ava told me her story, her eyes were wide and alive. She has a quiet voice and a round face, and sometimes her words came out sounding like she might start laughing at any moment, so great was her joy. She's in her fifties now, but as she talked about the dream she seemed like a little child.

Have you ever had an encounter with God that changed your life?

Read Acts 1 today. Try to put yourself in the place of the early disciples as they encountered the resurrected Christ, spent forty days with Him, and watched Him rise into the sky. Can you imagine how invigorated they felt at His appearance, how full of hope, how inspired? It was at the culmination of this forty-day appearance that Jesus offered these unforgettable words.

"You will be my witnesses in Jerusalem, and in all Judea and Samaria, and to the ends of the earth." (Acts 1:8)

There's something about the appearance of Christ that changes everything. Whether He appears in dreams or in person, whether He appears on a cross or in the clouds, the presence of Christ always brings transformation.

Your mission today is to do as the disciples did on that day after Jesus was taken up into the sky. What did they do? They gathered together and prayed.

Find at least one other believer today and pray together for the church in Iran. Pray that Jesus would appear in that country in many forms and that His appearance would bring about the same awakening that occurred in Jerusalem 2,000 years ago. Pray that Jesus would make Himself known to the people of Iran, through dreams and visions and the spoken word of His faithful people.

Pray that Jesus would appear to the country of Iran and that the trajectory of that nation would begin to shift.

ian. I have
and one br
en sick. I
my cousins.
rushed by
long for hope. Who can I talk to?
e into paradise? I can never please
ree but no job? I would like to marry and
say. Many of my peers use drugs to escape hopelessness.
What will happen to me if I change religions? S
become of my family? I am afraid I fee
I live in fear. On the Internet I see
tion is common. The love of Je
of my friends have
by the

DAY TWO

Ahmad

THE VISION

"In the last days," God says, "I will pour out my Spirit on all people. Your sons and daughters will prophesy, your young men will see visions, your old men will dream dreams."

ACTS 2:17

I'll never forget the day my brother came to my parents' house in a city south of Tehran, furious, his eyes wide and scary. It was soon after my father had died of cancer, and my mother didn't know what to do in the face of my brother's rage.

"I would beat you again, Ahmad," he said, "but you won't learn your lesson. So I will do the only thing I know to do. I will go to the government and tell them you have converted. I will let them deal with you."

I had become a Christian a few years before that, and it was a source of great shame to my family. Before he died, my father was an extremely devout Muslim, as was the rest of his extended family. He and my brothers had beat me many times because of my conversion. In any case, my brother was closely connected with the government, and he did what he said he would do.

Fortunately, on the day the government officials came to the house, I happened to see them coming from a long way off, so I ran away. My mother opened the front door for them (or else they would have broken it down), and they searched my room. That's when they found my Bible. I wonder if they read the notes I had written in it. I wonder if they read my favorite verse:

> "But what does it say? 'The word is near you; it is in your mouth and in your heart,' that is, the message concerning faith that we proclaim: If you declare with your mouth, 'Jesus is Lord,' and believe in your heart that God raised him from the dead, you will be saved. For it is with your heart that you believe and are justified, and it is with your mouth that you profess your faith and are saved." (Romans 10:8–10)

I don't know if they read any verses in my Bible, but they did make things very clear to my mother.

"Make sure he is here when we come back," they told her. But I never went back home. I ran away, this time to Tehran. I heard that the government officials went to my house every few weeks to see if I had returned. I was so worried—I didn't want to go to prison. So I called a Christian uncle on my mother's side who lived in Finland.

"I want to leave Iran," I told him. "I have to leave! But they invalidated my passport. I will never get out of this country!"

I'm sure he heard the panic in my voice.

"It's okay, Ahmad," he said quietly. "Everything will be okay. I know someone, a friend, who can smuggle you out. It's a short horse ride over the border, that's all. It's nothing to be afraid of. But it will cost you $1,000."

I took the money and went to the place my uncle had arranged. A Muslim man on a motorcycle picked me up. We didn't speak at all from the time I got on the motorcycle until we were out in the wilderness. It was a long ride that took many hours. Eventually, he hid me in the mountains, among the boulders and the shadows close to the Turkish border. It was around five o'clock in the evening.

"I'll be back in thirty minutes," he said with a warning in his voice. "Don't move from this spot, or I'll never find you and I won't come back."

So I sat there, and the weather began to get cold. I saw jackals trotting along, off in the distance. The sun sank beneath the horizon, and still the man didn't return. Three hours passed. I began to doubt him. After all, he was a Muslim. Why would he help me, a former Muslim converted to Christianity? It was more likely he had gone to tell the authorities. I was probably being set up! Four hours passed. Five hours.

Still, there I sat—a computer programmer lost in the wilderness. I didn't have survival skills! I didn't even know which direction to go to get to Turkey. I spent my days behind a keyboard, programming laptops, not fighting wild animals and living off the land. I didn't know what to do. I was so scared.

Jesus, I have faith in you, I prayed, but I don't think I can do this. I don't think I can go through with it.

I left my hiding place and began walking back down the mountain, back toward the closest village. What would I do when I got there? I had no idea, but I couldn't wait any longer. I was too cold, too unsure . . . too afraid.

But then I heard a voice in my ear.

Go back, the voice said. *I will take care of you.*

No, I said. *I don't think I can do it.*

Do it! Go back! I will take care of you.

I was confused and torn about what to do, but after ten minutes of walking I turned around. I found the place where the man on the motorcycle had hidden me, back behind the rocks, in the deep nighttime shadows.

He was there, waiting.

"Where were you?" he asked. "I was just about to leave."

He held the reins to two horses, and he handed one set of the leather straps to me.

"Never mind," he said. "It doesn't matter. Hold these."

"I've never ridden a horse before," I said. "How should I ride?"

He shrugged.

"Just hug the horse," he said, walking away. Then he looked back at me and, climbing up onto his horse, added, "And don't let go."

We rode through the night. The sound of the horses' hooves on the rocks and the ground was loud, and above us the stars were bright. Sometimes my horse would knock a small stone from the path and it would clatter down the side of the mountain. I wasn't cold any longer—it took all of my energy to stay on the horse, and it was hard work. It felt as if, with every movement, the horse was trying to jostle me off. The ground seemed very far below. Then I heard another sound.

Shouts rang out! Lights flashed up ahead! A vehicle revved to life, then beamed its sweeping headlights toward us.

"It's the border guard!" my guide hissed. "They're waiting at the crossing. Turn around! We'll have to find another way!"

I didn't know how to turn my horse around, but I didn't have to because at the next sound the horse turned on its own and hurried away: gunshots rang through the night. My horse followed my guide's horse as bullets shattered the rocks around us. I expected a bullet to break into my body at any second. I wondered what it would feel like. I wondered if it would hurt, or if I would die right away. I clung to my horse, it's mane blowing in my face, and I pleaded with God.

"I don't want to die here in the wilderness, on the border. Why did you bring me here, if only to die? I want to live! I want to serve you!"

We went to a second crossing, and there were guards there as well. We tried a third point, and again we had to flee from the border patrol. Finally, at the fourth gap in the mountains, we were able to get through. After three hours of riding, we crossed into Turkey. My legs and hands were bleeding, and my arms ached incredibly.

"I can't believe it," my guide kept saying. He was shocked. "I don't know how we are still alive. It's a miracle."

We arrived at a small town, and the villagers came running to see who we were. I collapsed on the ground, and they helped us, gave us water, and attended to my wounds. Eventually, a car took me to the city where I joined other Iranian refugees. After a short time, I found a small church in Turkey. They took me in until I could file the correct paperwork to go to the United States.

When I think back on that night, it's such a strong memory in my mind. But what sticks out the most isn't the smell of the horses or the sound of bullets whizzing over our heads. It's not the long wait for my guide to return, or our continued attempts to find a way through the mountains.

No, what I remember most is that voice I heard: *Go! I will take care of you.*

LIVE | DEAD CHALLENGE

Visions . . . dreams . . . prophecies, all three form a strong theme throughout the modern-day stories of Iranian Christians.

Ahmad is a thin young man with a gentle voice. When he talked about hearing God's voice, he spoke with a sense of awe.

Have you ever had a vision that gave you a greater understanding of Christ? Have you ever had a particularly lucid dream that impacted the way you live? Have you ever prophesied into the life of another human being, bringing them wisdom that wasn't of this world?

Read Acts 2 today. Imagine the courage it took for Peter to stand up and preach the gospel less than two months after Jesus' crucifixion. Consider the sermon he preached, the passages from Scripture that he quoted, and how these verses illustrate the power of the Holy Spirit when it is poured out on God's people.

Pray that your own community would experience this power. Pray that those who minister in and to Iran would experience Peter's courage. Ask if there are more ways that you can partner with those taking the gospel to the people of Iran. Consider your role in reaching the unreached people of the world: Are you to pray? Are you to give? Are you to go?

Finally, as in Acts 2, pray that as a result of these visions, dreams, and prophecies millions of Iranians will accept the message of salvation and be baptized.

I a...
three sisters...
Mother has been...
holidays with my cousin... I...
Muslim. I am crushed by Is...
Spiritual poverty. I long for hope. Who can I...
...lah. I have a degree but no job. I would like to...
...llah. God allow me into paradise? I can never...
...dren one day. Many of my peers use d...
...joyful. What will happen to me i...
...will become of my family?
...I live in fear. On the I...
...n is common. The...
...of my friends...
...by the...
...n fas...
cross...
A simp...
...e I do t...
My p...
...ght abo...
Jesus fo...

DAY THREE

Mariam

THE TRANSFORMATION

When all the people saw him walking and praising God, they
recognized him as the same man who used to sit begging at the
temple gate called Beautiful, and they were filled with wonder and
amazement at what had happened to him.

ACTS 3:9–10

The death of my son led me to God. But where do I begin telling such a story? How can a mother describe the heartache of losing her only son?

My husband didn't want our son to serve in the Iranian military, but it is mandatory there, so we talked about our options and looked for ways to leave the country permanently. My husband and I wanted to go to the United States, for the sake of our son and also our daughter, but we thought it would be easier for all of us to get visas if we applied through the Iranian embassy in Dubai. So we traveled to the UAE and put in our applications.

My husband's travel visa was approved. My travel visa was approved. My daughter's visa was approved.

But my son's was rejected.

It was an extremely difficult decision to make, but the three of us (my husband, my daughter, and I) went to the States and waited for my son there. He stayed behind in Dubai. Eventually he gave up on getting a US visa and applied to go to Turkey. His application was accepted, and he stayed with some extended family members there. I took a deep breath of relief because he wasn't alone any longer, and he wouldn't have to go back to Iran. At least not right away. For the time being, he was with family.

All the time he was there we worked with him to get him a visa to the US. When that didn't work out, he received a visa to travel to Sweden, and there he found a woman who took care of him as if he were her own son. By then I hadn't seen him for several years, but I was comforted to think that at least he was getting closer to us. He was moving farther west, farther away from the difficult life we had left behind.

Finally, when he was twenty years old, his visa was approved for the US. The painful separation came to an end! Our family felt whole again, and it was good. But as soon as he arrived, he was dissatisfied and quickly became depressed. He found it hard to make friends. He didn't hang out with people. He didn't go to parties. I watched him, and it made me sad that he couldn't find happiness.

My husband owned a gas station, and he convinced my son to work with him but our son didn't enjoy the work. In his loneliness, he found a new hobby: shooting guns. He got a permit and bought his own weapon. Twice a week he went to the shooting range, and the rest of the week he spent hours cleaning the gun, oiling it, and making sure it worked well.

I would go into his room and plead with him. "What is this that you have? Why do you need this gun? Is this the only hobby you can find? Get rid of it!"

But he didn't get rid of it. He spent more time shooting. He became more and more sad and isolated, and there was nothing I could do to draw out the boy I had known, my son. He missed his friends in Iran. He didn't like our new life in America.

One night, my husband and I were watching television in the living room while our eleven-year-old daughter sat quietly in her bedroom. Then it happened in one second. We heard a loud and terrible sound from our son's room. As we ran down the hall, our daughter dashed into the room ahead of us, into the smoke and the smell of burning flesh.

My son lay face down in a pool of his own blood. I marveled at how quickly it had happened, how quickly life had changed. He had placed the gun in his mouth and pulled the trigger. My daughter called the ambulance while my husband and I picked up that young man . . . my son . . . my boy . . . and wrapped him in a blanket. We carried him outside, to the steps, and waited for the ambulance to come. I held him in my lap. I rocked him back and forth.

I noticed first of all that his eyes were open and he looked up, up at the night sky high above the city. I felt for a pulse and imagined that I found it beating. I kept telling my husband, "He's going to live. He's going to be fine."

I heard the ambulance coming from far away, the siren wailing. The paramedics put our son in the ambulance, but instead of racing away they stood behind the vehicle and spoke for a few minutes. That's when I knew he was gone. That's when I knew my son was dead.

In our culture, after someone dies, the family sits for forty days. Friends and family come and visit, pay their respects, look after the immediate family, and say their own good-byes to the deceased. During those forty days, one of my friends, a Christian who had converted from Islam, came and sat next to me and prayed for me.

Every time she prayed for me, I felt a sense of peace. Every time she left me, she went to her church and told everyone there to pray for me, and every week the church prayed without knowing me. I had no idea this was going on.

In those long days after my son was gone I felt as though I had died as well. My insides felt withered, like a plant without water. I slept most of the day. Friends suggested I get help from a counselor, but I didn't listen. For two long years, I walked around the house, doing strange things, rubbing my hands together, and contemplating death. I wanted to die.

But my friend continued to pray for me, and one day she came back and visited my husband and me. I didn't want to talk to anyone, but she was there, so I let her in.

"Will you come with me to a Bible study on Friday night, Mariam?" she asked.

For two years I had not left the house, and there was my friend, asking me to go to a Bible study. I wanted to say no, but nothing came out. It was as if someone had covered my mouth. Before I knew it, I said, "Okay. I'll come."

Friday night arrived. My husband even came along with me. The first thing that caught my attention when we got there was the genuine love between the people. I know it was the love of Christ, and I saw it in each person there. They didn't know me, but everyone hugged me and cried with me for my son.

"Oh, Mariam," so many people said that night, "we're so sorry about your son. We've been praying for you for two years." When they prayed during the Bible study, the words stayed with me. Jesus began to heal me. He gave me a peace I had not felt since my son's death. I could sense His love.

I could feel myself coming back to life. The love of those Christian people and the love of Jesus drew me to God. That's how I came to believe in Jesus as my Savior. It was a difficult journey, but worth every step to find salvation.

LIVE | DEAD CHALLENGE

Mariam is a small woman. As she told me her story, her eyes pierced my heart. They held such a strong sense of sorrow, coupled with an all-encompassing peace. She couldn't tell her story without weeping at the sad parts, and laughing for joy when she talked about finding Jesus, about finding His peace.

While she told her story, those with us in the apartment kept interjecting.

"You wouldn't know her if you had seen her after her son died," they said. "She walked around like someone who was dead."

Read Acts 3 today and think how astonished the people in the town must have been when they saw the lame beggar walk and praise God! Make a list of the hopeless situations in your life: the relationships that seem broken beyond repair, the financial losses, the people who seem so lost. This is the beauty of Acts 3. The healing of the lame beggar shows that God's mighty power makes anything possible. Any transformation, no matter how unlikely, can take place when Jesus gets involved.

Now think about Iran. Many people, Christians even, consider Iran a lost cause, a place so steeped in corruption and religious manipulation that it could never experience a sweeping revival. But remember the healing that took place in Acts 3—a transformation that astonished everyone—and pray that Iranians throughout their country would experience the love of Christ. Pray that this would be a sign to the rest of the world of God's miraculous power.

ve
rother. My
I spend the
s. I was bo
n Islam. I
ope. Who a
radise? I can never please
job I would like to marry and
of my peers use drugs to escape hopelessness. I relig
happen to me if I change religions? Sometim
of my family? I am afraid I feel sad c
n fear. On the Internet I see others
s common. The love of Jesus s
of my friends have AIDS
by the cross
is require

Nahid

THE REVOLUTION

After they prayed, the place where they were meeting
was shaken. And they were all filled with the Holy
Spirit and spoke the word of God boldly.

ACTS 4:31

I became a Christian when I was seventeen years old while visiting a church in Iran that was celebrating the week of Pentecost. I never could have imagined the life that awaited me, how my husband (whom I had not yet met) would become a pastor of an Iranian congregation and spend time in prison. How my brother-in-law would be arrested for preaching in Farsi, the Persian tongue, and would not be allowed to leave Iran. How eventually my husband and I and our two children would flee the country.

But in 1972 that was far in the future. It was seven years before the Islamic Revolution, and people could still go to church freely. We filled the car with a group of neighborhood kids and drove to church, singing Christian songs loudly through the open windows. No one got upset about it. No one reported us to the government. There were no hardships because of our faith.

I was so hungry for the Word of God that I started attending multiple churches. I went to my home church, an Assyrian congregation, and then when that service ended I went to another church to hear an Armenian missionary speak. Someone translated his preaching into Farsi, which I understood better than Assyrian. I was so blessed to hear the Scriptures in that language.

While at that church I became friends with the youth pastor, Javed. He often taught from the Bible, and he sang very well. I went there for one to two years, and a mutual friend of ours told Javed that he had dreamed for three consecutive nights that we would be married. Neither of them told me this, but it was about that time that I began to have feelings for Javed.

We started hanging out and praying together, getting to know each other. He would come over to my house and teach a few of us Assyrian and English. I could speak Assyrian, but I couldn't write it well, so he helped me and my family with that. Soon after that we decided to get married. We both had secular jobs, but during the weekends and evenings he continued to volunteer in the youth ministry at the church.

Soon, the church asked him to leave his secular job and work full time in the ministry, so he did. There was a small bookstore next to the church, and he spent a lot of time there, hanging out with people from the community and telling them about Jesus. Then the church hired me, too, and my husband and I labored side by side for God's kingdom in Iran. I worked in the admissions office and mailed out information to interested pastors and missionaries who contacted us from all over the region.

We became deeply involved in the church, not just as believers who showed up on church days but as people whose very existence revolved around Jesus. We were thrilled to spend our lives spreading the gospel. It was so easy in those days, when we were free, but that freedom was about to come to an abrupt end.

I worked at the church until I was pregnant with my first child. That was when the protests began. Demonstrations against the Shah began in the fall of 1977 as students and religious Muslims took to the streets. Things only got worse in the beginning of 1978. When I took packets of information and other mail to the post office, I walked past people setting fire to tires or flipping over cars. One day I heard someone firing shots into the air. It was a loud, piercing sound, and I wondered where our country was headed. Still, we preached the gospel, and we waited to see what would happen next.

Two years after the Revolution took place, around 1981, our church asked us to move to another city to start a new church. Iran had become an Islamic state after the Revolution. School curriculums changed from secular to Muslim-based. As a woman, I had to cover myself when I went out in public. I had to make sure none of my hair showed from under my hijab where it encircled my face.

Iraq bombed one of Iran's airports just as we moved to start the new church. The Iran-Iraq War was one of the most violent wars since World War II, and it lasted eight years, from 1980 to 1988. Meanwhile, Islam solidified itself as the nation's one religion. Non-Muslims were considered second-class citizens, unable to attend most colleges or hold certain jobs.

In this hostile environment we started our first church, and it flourished. We decided that we wouldn't shrink away during difficult times but would continue to spread the gospel to the spiritually dead and hurting people around us. We proclaimed the name of Jesus boldly, and more and more people were added to our church. It was an amazing, exciting time to be a Christian.

LIVE | DEAD CHALLENGE

Nahid is strong and speaks with authority. When she talks about the way things were in Iran, it is in matter-of-fact tones. Her trust in Christ rises around her like a mighty fortress.

Acts 4 provides a beautiful story of the early church, small and vulnerable as a seedling, yet growing in spite of persecution. Thousands continued to hear the message and come to Christ in spite of threats, interrogations, imprisonment, and even executions.

This is mirrored by the Iranian church in the early 1980s, after the Islamic Revolution, and even up to today. But how do these churches flourish? How do they manage not only to continue, but even to grow, in the face of government resistance? There are at least three commonalities between the early church in Acts and the Iranian church: (1) they rely intensely on the Holy Spirit; (2) they proclaim the name of Jesus boldly; and (3) they interact as a community, holding nothing as personal property but sharing their possessions.

Think about your own church. Are you relying on the Holy Spirit? Are you proclaiming the name of Jesus boldly in your community? Are you reaching out to the poor, the widows, the hurting, and the spiritually dead?

Pray today that God would show you how to follow in the footsteps of these mighty Christians and that His spirit would show you how to engage in this movement to reach the unreached. Write five practical things you could do in your community to follow in the footsteps of the Iranian church . . . then do them.

I am Iranian. I have
three sisters and one brother. My
Mother has been sick. I
olidays with my cousins. I spend the
im. I am crushed by Islam
al poverty. I long for hope.
allow me into Par...
a degree ...
e day. Ma...
What w...
ll becom...
I live in fe...
tion is com...
ber of my ...
fascinated by ...
cross
I SOI...
Sometimes I read. Sometimes I don't sleep.
do not live
on the...

Arash

THE WHIPPING

They called the apostles in and had them flogged. Then they
ordered them not to speak in the name of Jesus, and let them go.

ACTS 5:40

My husband, Arash, loved to play soccer, and he often gathered the neighborhood children and young people for a game in the small grassy area close to our house. He would run around with them and laugh—all the children loved him so much. He was known for this.

One day, after playing soccer with the youth, Arash went with our son and his father to his father's paint shop. Often, the elderly men in the community met there to play dominoes, and sometimes the men brought alcoholic beverages to drink.

This particular day came during the month of Ramadan, a thirty-day period when strict Muslims fast during the day and eat only before sunrise and after sunset. Drinking alcoholic beverages is never permitted for Muslims, but during Ramadan

LIVE DEAD: THE STORY

it is particularly offensive. So someone, one of the neighbors perhaps, reported my father-in-law's shop as being a place where old men were drinking alcoholic beverages and were not observing Ramadan.

My husband had just arrived at the shop and was walking through the door with some friends when someone pushed him from behind. He turned and saw a large group of religious police. In Iran during that time, this was not something you wanted to see.

"What's going on here?" the police shouted. "Who owns this place?"

"It's my shop!" my father-in-law said. "It's my property, and we can do what we want here."

The police didn't agree. They grabbed everyone who was there, loaded them all into vans or buses, and drove them to the police station. One of the men who worked at the station happened to be good friends with my father-in-law, but when he saw him his face hardened.

"You don't know me," he hissed, turning away. "You don't know me."

They kept the men there for three days. My son was returned to me the first day. Then, on the third day, they released everyone except my husband and my father-in-law.

"It was me," my father-in-law insisted. "It was my shop. Why are you keeping my son here? Why don't you let him return to his job and his family?"

The person in charge of him in the prison gave him a haughty look.

"Father and son, father and son together," he said. "You've both blasphemed against religion, against holy laws."

So that became the charge used to hold them in prison: blasphemy.

My husband worked for a bank at the time, and he didn't want them to know that he had been arrested because he might lose his job. So I called and asked if he could have a few days off for vacation. They said that would be okay.

When I visited him on the third day, he told me that he would soon be whipped, and he asked if I could bring him some different clothes. He would be beaten with his clothes on, and he wanted to wear a thicker material, something that would help cushion the blows. So I brought him a sweatshirt and some sweatpants, and that's what he wore for the duration of his stay.

Sometimes I feel bad that I took those things to him, because it seems that the police beat him even harder when they saw that he wore thick clothes. They whipped him eighty times, and then they forced him to watch while they whipped his father eighty times. Afterward, they allowed both men to return to their homes.

When I first helped my husband take his shirt off, I couldn't bear to look at his back. It was entirely black from the bruising. A family member was visiting, but I wouldn't let her see it.

"It's too terrible," I said, shaking my head, tears streaming down my cheeks. "You don't want to see it. It's too awful."

I put olive oil on it many times each day and gently rubbed it into his bruised skin until his back glistened, shiny and now a deep purple fading to green around the edges. He tried not to make any sounds while I rubbed it, but I know it caused him a great deal of pain. I wondered if he would ever heal. I wondered if he would ever be the same again.

Soon after his whipping, he had a heart attack and spent two weeks in the Intensive Care Unit at our city's hospital. From that moment on, he always had heart issues, and I know this was the result of the beating. When we were finally able to move to the United States, he had open-heart surgery to repair some things that still weren't right.

Five years later, at the age of fifty-six, my husband passed away.

These are the memories I am left with when I think of my country, Iran, and all that we left behind. This is the pain that many people have been through. I love my country, and I pray every day that it can be a place of peace once again.

LIVE | DEAD CHALLENGE

When Arash's wife speaks of him, there is a deep sense of regret in her voice, as if she could have done something different. Perhaps if she hadn't brought in a sweatshirt they wouldn't have beaten him so furiously. I saw this in many of the Iranian Christians I met: not a regret that leads to despair, but a regret that desperately hopes things can be better.

Right now, as you read these words, people are being put into prison in Iran because they are Christians. Their captors beat them and torture them until they provide a list of the people who attend their church. Their captors insist they renounce their faith. Some have been killed or gone missing because they insist on preaching the gospel in Farsi or continue to hand out Bibles.

Every day, Iranian Christians must count the cost, not only for themselves but for their loved ones and their friends. If they continue to preach the gospel, they face a risk of being tortured or put into prison. *If they flee the country, their parents or siblings may be persecuted, followed, or have their phone lines tapped.*

Today, after you read Acts 5, pray that our persecuted brothers and sisters in Iran would feel the presence of God as never before. Pray that they would receive the strength to continue doing what God has called them to do.

Then ask Jesus how you can join in solidarity with them, whether this might be through faithful prayer or financial support for missionaries who are there or are going.

I am Iranian. I have three sisters and one brother. My ... has been sick. I spend the ... with my cousins. I was born ... crushed by Islam. I ... hope. Who ca... ? I can ... would li... peers us... en to me ... family ... On the ... on. The ... friends ... by the Cross ... I am ... appealing. A simple ... like I do some... I thought about pray... rested My countr... thought Jesus ... about Christ...

Sahar

THE PASTOR

But they could not stand up against the wisdom
the Spirit gave him as he spoke.

ACTS 6:10

'm twenty-eight years old now, and my family left Iran when I was eight. I don't remember much about my home country because I was so young when we left, but I do remember a little bit about my last year in school. I would have been in first or second grade. Islam was forced on us. In school we had to recite the Koran as well as say "Death to America" in the morning. A time was set aside in the daily agenda to pray to Allah and to read the Koran or other Islamic material.

Because I came from an Assyrian family and was not Persian like the majority of Iranians, the authorities let me step out of some of the religious lessons. A few Armenian children from my class would join me—they are one of the few minorities still allowed to practice Christianity in Iran, as long as they don't evangelize or perform their services in Farsi. So they speak Armenian in church, a language that, for the most part, only they understand.

My dad was a Christian pastor in Iran and was put in prison for his faith. I was much younger when that happened, but I heard the stories many times. When they took him we didn't know why. My mother had no idea where he was, so she started searching the hospitals and the morgues. The family called in favors and did what they had to do. Eventually he was released.

I don't remember much, but I remember the hardships. I remember walking down the street with my mother when I was a young girl, five or six years old. I wore shorts that went to my knees, and a man walking in front of us stopped, turned around, and started shouting in my face.

"Cover up! You're showing skin!"

I was shocked. My face turned white, then red with embarrassment. But he didn't stop there.

"What is wrong with you?" he screamed at my mother. "Go cover your daughter! This is offensive!"

My brother remembers more than I do about our years in Iran—he was fourteen or so when we boarded a plane for Turkey. He was afraid when we left the country, scared that the authorities wouldn't let us leave. There were stories about that, stories of families who were pulled off the plane at the last minute. I don't know if they were true, but leaving the country was a scary thing to do in the early 1990s. We had no idea how it would turn out.

Eventually, we ended up in Turkey. We were only there a few months, but I remember those days, how my parents worked with refugees, how my father traveled around and encouraged the churches of Istanbul. Some of the people who gave their lives to Christ during that time became pastors and traveled back to Iran. One of them is in prison right now.

From there we traveled to the United States, to southern California, and my father became the pastor of a church. I saw dozens of Iranians come to Christ at that church, Muslim converts. We never allowed anyone to take photos of their faces for fear the photos would find their way online and their families in Iran would be persecuted because of their conversion. The baptisms at that church, when people come up from under the water as new creations, were powerful. It was the first time I had been involved in helping lives transform so drastically. I wept for joy at those services.

As time passed, I realized that I wanted to be a pastor. I wanted to be part of that process of leading people to Christ, leading them from death to life, but so many people told me it would never happen.

"Sahar, a woman could never be a pastor in a Persian church," they would say. "It can't happen. Go study law or business. Make some money. There's no life for you in the ministry."

"I don't care," I said. "I really don't. I want to serve. I have experienced it, and I want to help others know Jesus."

So when I was twenty-five years old, I made the decision to become a pastor, no matter what my family said, no matter what anyone said. I began to study and meet with other women who had their credentials. I took classes one at a time. Initially my brother was my biggest opponent, but he became my number-one supporter.

The moment I received my ministerial credentials was life-changing. They arrived in a package the day before my birthday, and I felt the weight of responsibility as a pastor. I went to the store and bought a wedding ring and put it on my finger.

"God, I'm committed to you," I said as I put on the ring. "I'm committed to serving you."

My father passed away a few years ago, but I know he would be proud of me. I know he would be excited to see the growing number of Iranian Christians who are being baptized and are taking the gospel back to their friends and family in Iran.

LIVE | DEAD CHALLENGE

After speaking with Sahar for only a few minutes, I told her, "I think you're going to be a pastor someday." To which she replied, "I already am."

She spoke with the wisdom of one who is deeply grounded in Christ. We see this in Acts 6, when Stephen, though disrespected and falsely accused, still managed to speak with authority and power. No matter what arguments the people used against him, they could not come against the wisdom the Spirit gave him.

Because the Christians in Iran are constantly coming up against government opposition, they need an incredible amount of wisdom and discernment about what to say and how to say it. They need wisdom to know when to be subtle and vague, and when to speak clearly.

Pray today, first, that Christians in Iran would speak only out of the wisdom of the Holy Spirit. Then pray that their encounters with government officials would begin to transform the nation, and that those who seek to bring them down would be frustrated.

List three relationships or venues where you need to speak the truth of Christ with more boldness. Pray that the Holy Spirit would give you opportunities to do this and that you would join in solidarity with your Iranian brothers and sisters in Christ to proclaim the good news to the ends of the earth.

the
born a
I live in
this can I
I can never please
would like
peers use drugs to escape hopelessness. I read someth
pen to me if I change religions? Sometimes I
my family? I am afraid. I feel sad Christ
or. On the Internet I see others
common. The love of Jesus is very
friends have AIDS. I
by the cross

Ibrahim

THE EXECUTION

While they were stoning him, Stephen prayed, "Lord Jesus, receive my spirit." Then he fell on his knees and cried out, "Lord, do not hold this sin against them." When he had said this, he fell asleep.

ACTS 7:59–60

I recently heard the story of an Afghan man who was living in Iran. We'll call him Ibrahim. There are more than a million Afghans who live and work there, a lot of them having migrated south during the Soviet war in the 1980s. They speak basically the same language as Iranians do, although it has slight variations and is called Dari. Some Afghans are born in Iran, but people of Afghan heritage are not permitted to receive citizenship there, so even those who are born there are considered outsiders.

Ibrahim became a Christian in Iran after hearing an evangelist preach on the television. He was extremely sick, and his doctors gave him no hope for recovery, but while he watched the Christian television show he became saved and healed.

This just happened in the last year or so. He ended up coming to Turkey, where, for the first time, he saw a New Testament. Imagine reading the words of Paul for the first time, so close to some of the cities he had visited during his journeys.

About the time Ibrahim arrived in Turkey, his father and mother found out that he had converted.

"We don't have anything to do with him anymore!" his father exclaimed to his mother. "Do you understand? Your son is dead. He has denied the faith."

Time passed, and eventually Ibrahim was able to call back to Afghanistan to speak with his mother. She was so upset when she heard his voice on the telephone.

"How could this happen?" she asked. "How could you leave the faith?"

Ibrahim told her the story of how he had found Jesus. He talked about being "born again." When he used that phrase, she became silent.

"Mother, what's wrong?" he asked her.

She sighed.

"When I gave birth to you, I had a vision of an angel that came to me on a horse. The angel talked to me about being 'born again,' but I had no idea what the angel meant, and as the years went by, I put it to the back of my mind. But here you are, talking about being 'born again,' and now I finally understand what the angel was trying to tell me."

They spoke for a little while longer, and Ibrahim's mother professed faith in Christ.

Two months ago Ibrahim's father killed Ibrahim's mother after learning she had become a Christian. He burned her to death.

LIVE | DEAD CHALLENGE

I heard this story from an American man who lives and works in Turkey. He knows the people involved, and he knows firsthand the price that many Iranians pay when they decide to follow Jesus.

So many times we embark on a new journey with God only to turn back in fear or mistrust. We can't see how things will work out. We're not sure how the financial pieces will fall into place. We can't envision how God will provide.

Time and time again, both in stories about the early church and in stories from Iranian Christians, we see people who didn't let fear keep them from moving forward. After Stephen's stoning in Acts 7, I'm sure there were many who turned away from the faith. Their fear was simply too great.

Thankfully, the execution of Stephen didn't deter every Christian from moving forward in Christ. In fact, many more joined the Christians in spite of Stephen's death, perhaps because of it. The same can be said of our brothers and sisters in Iran— they are moving forward in spite of threats to their freedoms and their lives. Even after the interrogations, the beatings, and time in jail, they return to the streets and continue to share the gospel.

List the thing or things you believe God is calling you to do or be. Next to that list, make a list of the fears that keep you from moving forward with that call. Offer those fears to God and ask for courage.

Then, one by one, draw a line through each fear. Begin to focus on your call rather than on your fears. Trust that where God has called you, He will make a way for you.

I am Iranian. I have three sisters and one brother. My Mother has been sick. I spend the holidays with my cousins. I was bo... ...m. I am crushed by Islam. I... ...poverty. I long for hope. Wh... ...llow me into parad... ...degree but no job... ...day. Many... ...hat will... ...ecome of... ...e in fear... ...common... ...my friends... ...d by... ...e of Jesus is... ...oe others... ...ed. Christ... ...metimes I... ...I need somethi...

Mino

THE TEACHER

Then Philip ran up to the chariot and heard the man reading
Isaiah the prophet. "Do you understand what you are reading?"
Philip asked. "How can I," he said, "unless someone explains it
to me?" So he invited Philip to come up and sit with him.

ACTS 8:30–31

When I was a Muslim in Iran, I visited an Armenian church.
Because I was Muslim, I could not attend the regular
services, but I could go inside the church and look around, as a
tourist. So one day I did that.

The outside of the church was white, very beautiful, but it
also struck me as being rather lifeless. The large, plain walls rose
up against a pale blue sky. Inside, I saw all sorts of things I didn't
understand: paintings of men with circles around their heads;
shining, beautiful windows; many pictures of a woman in blue
holding a small child.

What I noticed most of all were the many crosses—these were strange symbols to me, considered blasphemous by my friends. Also, there were large scenes of the afterlife, heaven and hell, angels and demons. Standing inside that church made me feel strange, like I had entered another world, and I walked out with many questions.

Like many Iranians living in Tehran, I was a Muslim culturally but I didn't practice it as a religion. I studied the Koran from time to time, and I went to prayer services on the most holy days, but it wasn't something that impacted my life on a daily business. I went through the motions because everyone else was going through the motions. In fact, I was a bitter, angry person when I lived in Iran because I didn't like how the religious authorities tried to control everyone. I especially didn't like how women were treated.

I came to California because I wanted to visit, that's all. While I was here, a friend invited me to go to church, so I decided to go along.

"Don't talk to me about religion," I told the pastor before the service started, trying to be nice. "I don't believe in religion. I only believe that there is a God."

"Yes, yes, Mino," he said, smiling. "I understand. But soon you will see that your presence here is part of God's plan for you. You are here today because God brought you here."

I wasn't sure how to reply.

I decided to stay in the United States for a little while longer, and I started going to church on a regular basis. My Bible study teacher was always talking about Jesus. Jesus this and Jesus that. I had heard the name before, and I believed Jesus was a prophet, but nothing more than that. My teacher's constant references to Jesus got me thinking about Him a lot.

What I couldn't understand was how Jesus could be God. He was born, like us! Gods are not born. But as I continued to hear more and more things about Jesus, I started to wonder if perhaps it might be true.

For example, Jesus didn't do things like humans do. Even though He was tempted as we are tempted, He didn't pursue fame, money, wealth, or sex . . . none of those things. Even though He was tempted the same as we are, He never gave in. Also, when He performed a miracle, He didn't show off or say, "Look what I've done!" In fact, He often said the exact opposite: "Don't tell anyone what I've done."

I became a believer in January of 2013 and was baptized the following August. I became a new person. All the bitterness I felt towards people who had hurt me in the past evaporated. Even though none of my external circumstances changed, I was suddenly filled with a beautiful sense of peace.

This is what Jesus has done for me. I only needed someone to show me the truth.

LIVE | DEAD CHALLENGE

The story about Philip and the Ethiopian eunuch is one of the more incredible stories in the New Testament. Philip encountered a foreigner reading the Scriptures and explained to the man what he was reading. He baptized the man, then he mysteriously vanished and reappeared in another part of Israel.

Wow! That's pretty amazing!

LIVE DEAD: THE STORY

To me, the most telling part of the entire story took place when the Holy Spirit spoke to Philip, and Philip obeyed.

How often do we sense the nudging of the Holy Spirit, telling us to help our neighbor or encourage a stranger or tell a friend about Christ? How often do we listen to that still, small voice? And how often do we ignore it?

For the next three days, your challenge is to sit in silence for at least five minutes. Sit in complete silence—not while listening to music or driving the car. Spend five minutes in a quiet place while you do nothing else. During those five minutes, listen to what the Holy Spirit might want to say to you. When your mind wanders, and it will, simply whisper these words: "Give me wisdom, Holy Spirit."

Maybe He will lead you to explain the Scriptures to someone, as Philip did. Perhaps He will guide you to invite someone to church, as Mino's friend invited her. Perhaps the Holy Spirit will simply say, "Wait."

That's your challenge for the next three days.

Listen.

Mother ... holidays with ... Muslim. I am a crus ... Spiritual poverty. I long fo ... Will God allow me into paradi ... Allah, I have a degree but no job ... I would like to h ... children one day. Many of my peers use drug ... joyful. What will happen to me if I ... What will become of my family? I a ... ful. I live in fear. On the Inter ... tion is common. The love ... of my friends have AIDS ... by the Cross ... I am ... appealing ... like I do ... My ... about Jes ...

Ahmad

THE CONVERT

"Who are you, LORD?" Saul asked.
"I am Jesus, whom you are persecuting," he replied. "Now get up
and go into the city, and you will be told what you must do."

ACTS 9:5–6

I was born into a strict Muslim family. My father was a devout Muslim, a Haji. He had made many pilgrimages to Mecca, always during the proper times and strictly observing all of the rules and requirements. My grandfather was also extremely devout. I grew up doing the prayers and reading the Koran from a very young age.

Then a terrible thing happened to our family (or at least we all thought it was terrible at the time): my mother's brother, my uncle, became a Christian. He lived in a different city, and every once in a while we visited him. I thought poorly of him by that time. I thought he was weak and a disgrace to the family name.

One day, while we were visiting this uncle, he took me along to church. I was perhaps eight years old. As soon as we walked into the church, I started making fun of the people there . . . the way they closed their eyes when they sang, the way they raised their hands. I thought they were out of their minds, and their poor, little religion seemed so small to me, especially when compared to the great religion of Islam.

After the service I talked to my uncle.

"I will find everything that's wrong with Christianity," I told him. "I will explain to you why your religion is not enough."

By the time I was ten years old, I had read the Bible many times. I was constantly looking for things that might be wrong or that didn't make any sense. But in the meantime, I had also begun to examine the Islam of my father and my brothers. I realized that Islam offered nothing new or exciting. I saw no signs of the miracles I read about in the Bible.

So I became an atheist for five years, from the time I was ten until I turned fifteen. Christianity felt foreign to me, and Islam didn't make any sense. I decided there was no God. I was training to become a computer programmer, and my thoughts were totally logical, very straightforward, and for a little while that was enough . . . but not for long.

I kept thinking there must be more. There had to be something out there. Something! I went back and read the Bible; over and over again I read through it. Then one night I read Romans 10:8–10, a section I had read many times before: "But what does it say? 'The word is near you; it is in your mouth and in your heart,' that is, the message concerning faith that we proclaim: If you declare with your mouth, 'Jesus is Lord,' and believe in your heart that God raised him from the dead, you will be saved. For it is with your heart that you believe and are justified, and it is with your mouth that you profess your faith and are saved."

I read those words and started to tremble. The words in those verses overcame me. There it was. That was my answer!

"You are the Lord, Jesus," I just kept saying over and over again. "You are God."

My sister lived in another city and the two of us became Christians at the same time without knowing it. I started taking my Bible to school so I could read it during the day; I wasn't trying to disprove it, but to learn from it. My teachers found out about my Bible, so they called my father. He came to school and took me home.

"How could you do this?" he shouted. "What is wrong with you?"

He beat me that day, but I didn't fight back because I was a Christian and also because he was my father. The next day he told my brothers what had happened, and they came to the house to make sure I wouldn't fight back and hurt him. While they were there, I told them why Islam was wrong and why Christianity was so beautiful. The two of them beat me.

I ran away to my sister's house and stayed with her until things calmed down. Then my father was diagnosed with cancer, and as his health got worse and worse I decided I had to return home. It was a difficult decision to make, and I returned with great fear.

"You won't get hurt," my father insisted. "There will be no persecution. I just want you here with me before I die."

I spent one year in my father's house, and no one said anything to me about being a Christian. In fact, because I didn't want to upset my father while he was so sick, I kept quiet about it. My family began to think I had converted back to Islam.

After my father died, my brother found out I was still a Christian and he threatened to tell the government authorities. That's when I ran away for the final time, crossed the northern border on horseback, and arrived in Turkey.

After I found a church in Turkey, they asked if I would help with worship by playing the guitar. I was a novice musician, but I got up front and helped. I've never been musically talented, and I stumbled through each song, sometimes hitting the wrong chord, sometimes playing a little off-key.

That's when I remembered my first time in a church, how I had made fun of the people who were worshipping God. Now I was standing in front and leading worship, closing my eyes, and singing. I was doing the exact things I had ridiculed as a boy!

Sometimes I'm sure God has a great sense of humor.

LIVE | DEAD CHALLENGE

One of the major themes of Acts is that there is no such thing as a lost cause. God has the ability to soften even the hardest heart. He has a way of bringing the least likely people into the fold.

Nowhere is this more obvious in Acts than in the transformation of Saul to Paul. Jesus confronted the very man who led the persecution of the early church, and his heart changed. The man who stood by and watched the stoning of Stephen, the man to whom the executioners went and paid homage after Stephen's death, this man fell to the ground and cried out to God.

Your Live | Dead challenge today is threefold. First, practice your second day of silence. For at least five minutes, listen for the voice of Christ. If five minutes pass quickly, consider remaining silent for ten minutes or thirty minutes. It is in this quiet space that you can hear the voice of God most clearly.

The second part of the challenge is to think of the lost causes in your life, the disappointments and the broken relationships. Know that even the things that seem lost can be found again in Christ.

Finally, open yourself up to the possibility that God is about to lead you in a different direction. Perhaps the thing you said you would never do is the thing God wants you to do. Perhaps you said you'd never be a pastor. Perhaps you said you'd never start a small group. Perhaps you said you'd never be a missionary.

Ahmad never imagined he would lead worship in a Christian church. Paul never imagined he would follow Christ. Open yourself up to the transformational power that Jesus Christ offers.

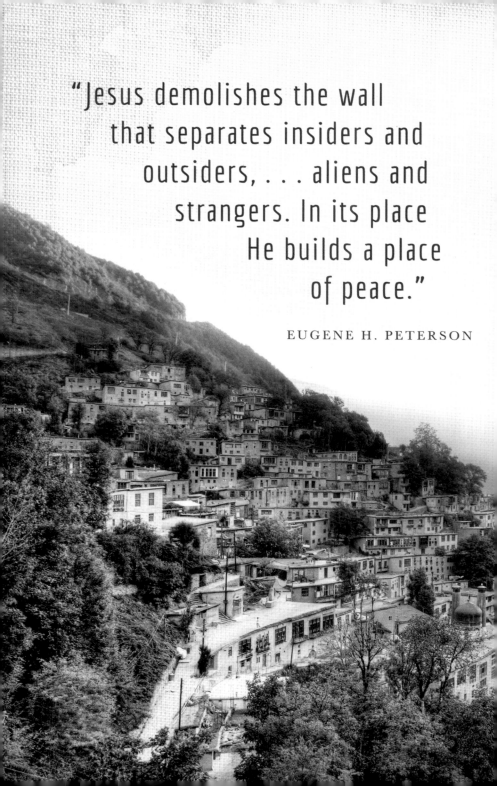

"Jesus demolishes the wall
that separates insiders and
outsiders, . . . aliens and
strangers. In its place
He builds a place
of peace."

EUGENE H. PETERSON

I am Iranian. I have
three sisters and one brother. My
Mother has been sick. I spend the
holidays with my cousins. I was born
in. I am crushed by Islam. I was born in
poverty. I long for hope. Who will take me to
allow me into paradise? I can never please
a degree but no job. I would like to mi
day. Many of my peers use drug
What will happen to me if
become of my family?
live in fear. On th
n is common

Leyla

THE UNCLEAN

Then Peter began to speak: "I now realize how true it is that God does not show favoritism but accepts from every nation the one who fears him and does what is right."

ACTS 10:34–35

I was eleven years old when the Islamic Revolution took place, and that was followed by the war against Iraq. I don't have very good childhood memories. Airplanes flew high over the city and dropped bombs close to our house. One landed in our neighborhood. I remember how people from the Iranian Army rushed us to bomb shelters, and how we huddled there in the dark, listening for explosions, wondering if our lives would end.

Before the revolution, boys and girls went to school together, but after the revolution we had separate schools through high school. In the university we could be together, but the girls had to be completely covered. Before the revolution, everyone in my family was extremely religious, but after the revolution only my uncle remained religious. Everyone else got tired of religion being forced on them.

When I was in my thirties, I started a beauty salon in my apartment. It was a wonderful place where my female friends and customers could come and take off their burkas and their hijabs and just be themselves. Men couldn't come in, and when the women came to get their hair cut they could relax and simply be women. We laughed and cried together in that salon. It was a good place. But when they left at the end of their appointment, they had to cover themselves completely.

I moved to the United States in 2005 because my sister and my mother already lived there. I started attending an Iranian church because I was so homesick for Iran. I missed my wonderful family who remained in Iran, and I missed the culture and history of my city.

But here in America I found my Jesus, and He has filled me with a peace and a love that I cannot understand. When I call Him "my Jesus" friends smile, but that's how I feel about Him. Before He became my Savior, I was sad and angry at the people who had ruined my country. Now, I know that things can change there for the good.

There are many misconceptions about the Iranian people. I don't think the average American even knows that a variety of people live in Iran: 50 percent are Persian, 25 percent are Azeri (Turkic), and the rest are smaller groups like Kurds, Turkmen, Baloch, Arabs, Armenians, and Assyrians. It's a country with rich cultural ties for all these ethnicities and one that has an interesting and long history.

Many Americans also think Iranian women are docile and uneducated, but that's not true: many are engineers, doctors, and college professors. Women make up 60 percent of the college students in Iran. Women can drive in Iran. Women can vote. I'm not saying things are perfect in Iran for women, but they have many freedoms and opportunities. There are also kind Iranian men who take care of their families and work hard. Not everyone who converts to Christianity is persecuted by their family—many families support their children, even if they become Christians.

Some of my American friends think Iran is a desert, but it's actually quite a beautiful country. Tehran gets a lot of snow each year and has four seasons.

Iran is a place I pray for every day.

Will you pray with me?

LIVE | DEAD CHALLENGE

What comes to mind when you think of Iranians? For most Americans, the word that comes to mind is terrorist *or* Muslim. *There is often a sense that the Iranians are a lost cause or are beyond help. But the beautiful thing about Acts 10 is Peter's realization that nothing and no one is beyond God's love. This is what he expressed after his vision: "The voice spoke from heaven a second time, 'Do not call anything impure that God has made clean'" (verse 9).*

Are there people in this world you consider unclean or unfit to hear the gospel? People who disagree with you politically? People who are dedicated to a different religion? Iranians?

In the book of Acts, God consistently asks His people to expand the boundaries of their love. Today, during your third day of silence, ask Him to show you who currently fits into your category of "unclean." Then ask Him to open your heart to the existence of those people around you, and begin to look for opportunities to serve them.

Finally, pray that God would soften your heart to the Iranian people. If you cringe or bristle at the term Iranian, ask that the Holy Spirit would replace your feelings of fear or negativity with an overwhelming sense of compassion and a knowledge that each Iranian is loved deeply by God.

I am crushed by ... I spend the ... I was born ... my ... erty I long for hope. Who can I talk to? ... me into paradise? I can never please ... gree but no job. I would like to marry ... y. Many of my peers use drugs to ... at will happen to me if I ... ... of my family? ... e in fear. On the I H ... s common. T ... f my friends ... d by the ... ss ... I ... AIDS is ... ...

AS TOLD BY ZARINA

DAY ELEVEN

Hassan

THE DISCIPLE

Then Barnabas went to Tarsus to look for Saul,
and when he found him, he brought him to Antioch.
So for a whole year Barnabas and Saul met with
the church and taught great numbers of people. The
disciples were called Christians first at Antioch.

ACTS 11:25–26

When my husband and I still lived in Tehran, he brought a man home with him at the end of the day. This man was a drug addict. I had never seen or met a person who was addicted to drugs. I knew something was wrong with him as soon as he walked through the door, but I couldn't have told you what. I didn't even know what the word *addict* meant.

"There is no one who will take care of this man," my husband explained. "He just gave his heart to the Lord, and if we let him go, he will return to his old lifestyle."

So we brought him into our home. It was 1979, and our first child, a boy, was born during that time. The first addict who came into our home was named Hassan. His lip was torn right down the middle with jagged, worn stitches holding it together. A long piece of the stitching had come loose, and the string hung down from his lip. It wriggled when he spoke.

All of his fingertips were burned, and my husband later told me that his chest had burn marks on it from falling asleep with cigarettes in his mouth. They would drop from his lips while he slept, eventually burning through his shirt and scarring his skin.

At first we put him in our own bed. Months later he shared in front of our church, with many tears, that he had never before in his life slept in a bed with white sheets. During the rare times when he had a home, he slept on the floor, and when he was on the streets he slept in telephone booths or in the gutters. If he was lucky, he would find a large piece of cardboard and sleep in a sheltered place on the sidewalk.

One night my husband said something to me while the two of us sat together in our bedroom.

"God showed me something when I first met Hassan on the street," he said.

"Yes?" I asked.

My husband turned and looked deep into my eyes.

"God told me that the first addict I bring home will serve Him faithfully for the rest of his life."

After Hassan, my husband brought four more men to live at our house, all heroin addicts. They came to our home looking lost and hurt, and we did our best, without any medical training, to rehabilitate them and put them on God's path.

My husband's parents also lived with us, as well as his younger sister. We lived in a two-bedroom apartment, so it was me, my husband, my newborn, my father and mother-in-law, my sister-in-law, and five drug addicts—eleven of us. My in-laws and my sister-in-law shared a bedroom. My husband and I slept in the other bedroom with our baby boy. All of the recovering addicts slept in the living room.

The eleven of us shared a shower, and I washed everyone's clothes by hand. We became a family, a close-knit family, and as each of the drug addicts got clean and began to follow God's path for their lives, they returned to their families. When our denomination called us to start a church in another city, we moved from Tehran. By then, only one addict remained in our house, and he moved with us, staying with us for three more years.

In our new city, my husband decided the best way to gather people in our new church was to spend his days in the Square of the Shah (the square of the king). He set up a table with Bibles and all kinds of books about Christianity. The last recovered addict, the one who had gone with us to this new city, helped my husband in everything that he did. He would sometimes take care of the table himself, even though by then the Revolution had occurred and it wasn't safe to be a Christian. He would stand at that little table and shout, and his voice reverberated throughout the square.

"This is the gospel of Jesus!" he cried out, holding up a Bible. "This is the gospel of the Messiah who brings salvation!"

With the help of that recovered addict, we built up God's church in that city.

And what became of our first recovered addict, Hassan? He is married with children and to this day serves God as a pastor in Iran. One of the other former addicts is a pastor in northern California. A third is currently in an Iranian prison for teaching about Jesus.

This is what God does. He uses the people who are least in the eyes of society to glorify His kingdom and to draw people to Himself.

LIVE | DEAD CHALLENGE

Another major theme in Acts is discipleship, the practice of Christians to live intentionally alongside each other. In today's reading we see that for an entire year Paul and Barnabas met together with the church in Antioch. Isn't it interesting that out of this partnership, this discipleship, the people who followed Jesus were first called Christians? Discipleship is foundational to Christianity.

Today's challenge is to think about your life as a Christian. Are you living it alone? Are you walking a lonely road? Try to think of another Christian who could share life with you, someone you could meet on a regular basis to encourage and challenge each other. Perhaps you could consider going through this book with that person, engaging in the challenges together.

When Paul and Barnabas began meeting together with the church in Antioch, the word Christian came into being. When this Iranian pastor took a heroin addict named Hassan into his home, he not only changed Hassan's life but the lives of countless others whom Hassan led to Christ. Who are you impacting for Christ?

Finally, pray for the scattered believers in Iran whose churches are closed and who are being watched by the government. Pray that they would still sense communion with the body of Christ, and that God would provide fellow believers to encourage them.

Many of my peers... no job? I could like to marry and... Who said I talk to? I can never please... will happen to me if I change... use drugs to escape... I am afraid... of my family? I am afraid... fear. On the Internet I see others... friends have... love of Jesus... I feel sad. Sometimes... sad. (I

Ali

THE ARREST

He had James, the brother of John, put to death with the sword.
When he saw that this met with approval among the Jews,
he proceeded to seize Peter also.

ACTS 12:2–3

The day my husband, Ali, answered the phone and told the man seeking Christ where we lived was the day our lives in Iran changed. The person who called wanted to know more about Jesus, so Ali gave him our home address and told him to come over. Of course we knew this was dangerous, but my husband would never have been willing to risk turning away someone who was genuinely interested in learning about God.

We answered the knock on the door, and there were two men standing there, not one. When they came into our house, they looked everywhere and asked many questions.

"Why don't you have a seat?" Ali asked the men, and then he asked me to bring them some water. But they didn't sit. They took a Bible off of his table, flipped through the pages and read his notes, then went through every book on his shelves, one by one.

"You should go get dressed," they said in flat voices without even looking at him. "We need to go."

That's how I found myself in the bedroom with my husband while he prepared to leave. My son was in school and my daughter was very young, around one year old.

"They're going to take me away," my husband said in a calm voice. "Once we are gone, take the books that are under the bed and bury them in the ground at our friend's house."

He said this because he owned some books that spoke poorly of Islam, but he never kept them with the rest of his library. He dressed slowly in his suit. He put on the clerical collar all pastors in Iran were expected to wear so that they could be easily identified. He picked up a fresh Bible, one with no markings in it, and he started walking out the bedroom door. But then he stopped, and he spoke to me.

"Be careful with the children," he said, "and with the church of God."

Then they took him away.

I spent the first night pacing through the house, then walking out into the front yard before going back inside. I kept expecting to hear the doorbell. Perhaps they would bring him home. Perhaps they would come back to tell me he was dead. Or perhaps they would take me away, too. Then what would happen to the children? What would they do with our children? What would happen to our church, the people we loved as brothers and sisters? There were so many questions, so much uncertainty.

The next morning I walked outside, still pacing. I hadn't slept all night. I saw a blue car parked on the street with two gentlemen inside, observing our house. I went back in and called a friend of mine who was a doctor and a Muslim who had converted to Christianity. She came over with some of our other friends, and we prayed together. The voices of God's people were soothing to me. Then the church's board members came over, and we decided to spread out and visit every hospital, prison, and mortuary in town, just to see if we could find out what had happened to my husband.

I put my son in school, and one of the deacons of the church drove my daughter and me to eight mortuaries in our city. None of them had heard of my husband. This gave me hope that he was still alive. We called the hospitals and even contacted the religious courts to see if he had been tried. No one would tell me where my husband was. Perhaps none of them even knew.

Every night we gathered with the church, and we prayed and prayed. The husband of the first lady who had come to the house was a dentist who worked on Islamic leaders. He said he would ask subtle questions and try to find out where my husband had been taken.

After one week, one of his patients told him that my husband was alive and in prison, but we still had no idea where he was being kept. Was he in our city? In another city? What would become of him? On the fourteenth day of his absence, the telephone rang.

It was Ali.

"Ali, why is your voice so raspy?" I asked him.

"I haven't spoken in many days," he said, "perhaps not even since I left. They have asked if I can post bail. That way I can leave prison until my case is processed."

I was overjoyed. One of our friends who had a store wrote up the paperwork to cover my husband's bail. We picked him up from the prison, and he looked like a different person. The time in the prison had affected him.

He said that at first he had been completely blindfolded and they had shouted their charges at him. *You preach to Muslims! You give Bibles to Muslims! You shouldn't do these things!*

After the endless charges, during which they never allowed him to speak, they put him in solitary confinement for three days. There was no light, no window. He sat in complete darkness for three days. No one spoke with him. They slid food to him under the door at the appointed times. Then they brought him out again, blindfolded, and asked him the same questions, this time demanding that he put his answers in writing.

One month after his release, his trial took place. They called our house and then came to pick him up again. He was blindfolded and taken away, and I didn't know if I would see him later that day, or the next day, or the next week . . . or perhaps never again. No one would tell us anything.

He appeared before the supreme judge of our city. The only thing they asked him was, "Why do you give out Bibles?"

My husband stood quietly before them, still blindfolded, and answered.

"I am a pastor and my job is with the Bible. If I was a shop owner, I would sell you nail clippers, or food, or a broom. But because my job involves the Bible, I hand out Bibles. Is it so wrong that I do this thing that simply has to do with my job?"

After some time, they told him to leave.

"Just go," they said. "Go home. We are finished with you here."

"But I don't know how I got here. I was blindfolded. Where am I? How am I to get home?"

At that point they removed the blindfold, and he saw in front of him a file with his name on it, several inches thick. There was even a photograph of him from the day of his ordination, and he knew at that point that the people who had brought charges against him were people from inside our own church. There were people in our own congregation trained to gather information and build a case.

He returned home, and we continued our work for God in that city.

LIVE | DEAD CHALLENGE

One common trait of the individuals we interviewed for this book is perseverance. They don't give up. They keep moving forward. They continue to proclaim the love of God.

This is also one of the main traits found in the stories of the early church. Ridiculing crowds didn't deter them. The death of Stephen only caused the church to grow even more. And in Acts 12, the death of James, and Peter's imprisonment, only caused the church to pray harder and to seek God more earnestly.

The question we must ask ourselves is this: How easily are we discouraged? How quickly do we give up? And how much do we miss when we don't persevere to the end?

Today, take some time to journal about areas of your life where you feel discouraged, where you are on the edge of giving up. Then ask God for the strength to keep going. Pray that the Christians in Iran would persevere.

ther. My
I spend th
I was bor
Islam. I
hope. Who can I talk to?
paradise? I can never please
no job I would like to marry and
many of my peers use drugs to escape hopelessness. I read
what will happen to me if I change religions? Someti
will become of my family? I am afraid I feel sad
I live in fear. On the Internet I see othe
on is common. The love of Jesus
my friends have A
jo by the C

Nasrin

(PART ONE)

THE LAW

Therefore, my friends, I want you to know that through Jesus the
forgiveness of sins is proclaimed to you. Through him everyone
who believes is set free from every sin, a justification you were not
able to obtain under the law of Moses.

ACTS 13:38–39

I grew up in Iran in an extremely religious family. My father
and his extended family were especially devout Muslims. So
as I grew older and reached my teenage years it was crucial
that I always covered myself before I went outside the house,
with no hair showing where my hijab lined my face. I couldn't
wear makeup or do my nails or trim my eyebrows (and I had
bushy eyebrows). Any of those things would have been shameful
behavior, especially for someone who wasn't yet married.

When I was fifteen years old, my father promised me in
marriage to a thirty-year-old man I had never met. That didn't

shock or horrify me—it just seemed like another step in my life. I would get married and have children and life would go on. So I prepared to get married, and while I was a little nervous, I was also excited about starting a new chapter in my life.

We got married in a government office and, as usual when going out in public, I wore a hijab so that only my face was exposed. I was so shy and uncertain that I didn't say a word during the entire ceremony. At the end of the brief meeting, we got our license and had a small party at my parents' house, just to show people we were married.

That was it. I had a husband. I wasn't afraid of being married. I had no reason to be. I guess I had no idea what to expect. Everything was okay for a few months, but pretty soon my husband became agitated. He seemed nervous when I was around, and he wouldn't speak to me about anything. I tried to talk to him, but he was so quiet, and I began to sense a deep layer of anger inside of him. It frightened me.

One night I approached him in his bedroom—we had separate rooms. I thought that since we were married, we should talk, right?

"I would like to talk to you," I said hesitantly. But he looked at me with disgust.

"No," he said. "Get out and shut the door."

Soon after that he started beating me. We would get into arguments, and he would hit me, or I would do something wrong and he would push me into the wall. Sometimes he did these things for no reason at all. I couldn't talk with my mom or my sister about it. I was quiet, and I kept it in all inside my heart.

As the weeks and months passed, I became a hateful person. I hated his family. I hated strangers I passed in the street.

But I hated my husband more than anyone else, and this hate grew and grew inside of me. I started telling him I hated him, right to his face, but this only gave him more excuses to beat me.

Finally I cried out to Allah. *God,* I cried out, *where are you? Can't you help me? Where are you?*

But everything was silent, and I came to the conclusion that Allah was angry with me for something I had done wrong, some long-ago sin or mistake. In Islam, God always seemed angry to me, and I always felt that with one misstep He would kill me or send me straight to hell.

I went from being an active, joyous girl to an isolated, angry woman with no friends. I didn't reach out to people, and my family never came to my house for meals. My life got worse and worse, and I thought about killing myself.

God, I kept crying out, *where are you?*

But I heard nothing.

LIVE | DEAD CHALLENGE

I met Nasrin in the Midwest. These days she has a beautiful smile and an outgoing personality. When she told her story, she seemed to be talking about someone else, sharing the details of a girl she had once known. There was wonder in her voice, as if she couldn't fathom the pain of someone forced to go through such terrible things.

But she had gone through them. And there she was, sitting across from me in an American coffee shop, sometimes laughing, sometimes wiping tears carefully from the corners of her eyes.

"Therefore, my friends, I want you to know that through Jesus the forgiveness of sins is proclaimed to you." (Acts 13:38)

What a beautiful proclamation, and something Paul says was not attainable under the law of Moses. Yet so many in the world still believe they live under the law. They strive to say enough prayers, attend enough meetings, fast during the required fast days, do enough good things, and in so doing hope to gain the favor of God.

Even with the miraculous growth of the church in Iran, the vast majority of Iran's seventy-nine million people have never had the opportunity to escape enslavement to the law. They have not heard the gospel.

Today, spend some time journaling and writing about what it would look like for you to join the effort of spreading the gospel to the nation of Iran.

other. My
I spend th
s. I was born a
Islam. I live in
hope. Who can I talk to?
paradise? I can never please
no job. I would like to marry and
any of my peers use drugs to escape. hopelessness. I read
What will happen to me if I change religions? Someti
I live in fear. On the Internet I see othe
of my family? I am afraid. I feel sad
is common. The love of Jesus
by the C
of my friends have A

DAY FOURTEEN

Nasrin

(PART TWO)

THE MISCARRIAGES

Then some Jews came from Antioch and Iconium and won the crowd over. They stoned Paul and dragged him outside the city, thinking he was dead. But after the disciples had gathered around him, he got up and went back into the city.

ACTS 14:19–20

There were ten people who lived in that house: my husband, his mother, his siblings, and their spouses and children. My schedule, every day (because I was the newest daughter-in-law and didn't have any children) was to wake up at 6 a.m. each morning. Some mornings it was so cold that the water made my hands numb. Then I prepared for breakfast, made the food, cleaned up the dishes, washed all the clothes and linens by hand, made lunch, cleaned the house, made dinner, cleaned up after dinner, and then prepared for the next day.

My mother-in-law told me often how spoiled I was because my father was rich, and she took it as a personal challenge to break me down, to humiliate me as much as possible. She woke me every morning, without exception.

Wash the dresses, make the food, serve the food, do the dishes. Every day was the same as the day before. *Where is my dream?* I thought to myself. *Since when is this what life is all about?* I had always wanted to be a singer or an actor. I thought I could work in TV or theatre or in the movies, but there I was, slaving away from sunup to sundown.

That's when something inside of me died: my hope for a good life, happiness, and my faith in God. After two years of marriage, you wouldn't have recognized me compared to the young girl I had been before marriage. I was bitter, hard, and angry, and I was only seventeen years old. My tongue was sharp. If I talked to you, I hurt you.

But then something happened, something that would change me.

I got pregnant.

My family had told me that if I got pregnant and could give my husband's family a child, things would change. I would be happier. They would know my body was healthy. It often felt to me like a woman's body was simply for sex and having children and serving around the house. If I could have a healthy child, I thought they might love me.

I was tired of being a servant. I wanted to be appreciated as a person. I thought that if I told my husband I was pregnant, he would love me. But he only hated me more.

"I don't want a baby from you," he said. "You disgust me. Why would I want to have a child with you?"

I miscarried my first child, giving birth in my bedroom in the house.

Then I miscarried my second child, and still my husband wouldn't take me to the hospital.

Finally, I miscarried a third time, my body giving up that small mass of bloody tissue shaped like a baby. I wept.

Through all of it, my husband never took me to the hospital. I lost those babies at home, and I was so sad, but he never asked me how I was doing. He never made sure I was recovering properly. By that time, I rarely left my room. I had been married for four years.

I so badly wanted to have a baby. In my mind, having a baby had become the solution to all of my problems. If I could get pregnant again and carry the baby full term, perhaps then they would love me and my life would get better.

I spoke to my father.

"Daddy," I said, "I need help."

He didn't want me to get a divorce because that would be shameful for him, so he said he would help me. He took me to the doctor, and once I entered my fourth pregnancy, my father took me home to stay in his house throughout the pregnancy. My family put me on bed rest, and I didn't have to serve anyone else. I was so happy. I could just sleep and eat and wait for the baby to be born.

I lived with my parents for all nine months of my pregnancy. I cut my hair short and didn't even get up to shower. My father took such good care of me. Then I went into labor.

LIVE | DEAD CHALLENGE

Acts 14 is an incredible story of a near-death experience for Paul. He was stoned by the crowd, dragged outside of the city, and left for dead. But the most telling part of the story is in verse 20: "But after the disciples had gathered around him, he got up and went back into the city."

"After the disciples gathered around him" sounds much like what happened to Nasrin. After three miscarriages, she was close to death. But in her fourth pregnancy, she managed to carry a baby for nine months after her father brought her into his own house: "after her family gathered around her."

One of the major hallmarks of the early church was a willingness to gather around others to help them. In order to live dead, we must put the needs of others above our own needs and desires.

Make a list of friends from your church or community who need someone to gather around them. Can you take them a meal? Can you babysit their children? Can you meet to pray with them? Can you give them financial aid?

Take the Live | Dead Challenge from Chapter Eight one step further. Become a person who gathers with others around those in need. And gather with others in prayer around our Iranian brothers and sisters. You could be, as those early disciples were for Paul, the crowd that gathers around and sees a resurrection.

...ther. My...
...I spend th...
...I was bor...
...Islam. I...
...hope. Who can I talk to?
...paradise? I can never please...
...no job. I would like to marry and
...any of my peers use drugs to escape hopelessness. I read
...happen to me if I change religions? Someti...
...become of my family? I am afraid. I feel sad
...I live in fear. On the Internet I see othe...
...on is common. The love of Jesus...
...of my friends have AI...
...by the C...

Nasrin

(PART THREE)

THE VOICE

When they came to Jerusalem, they were welcomed by the church and the apostles and elders, to whom they reported everything God had done through them.

ACTS 15:4

After losing three babies, I finally had a healthy baby boy. He was close to eight pounds, and I couldn't stop looking at him. He was just so beautiful . . . so perfect. Seeing him there, I thought, *Now everything will change.*

Having a boy in my culture was a big deal. I thought I had saved my life by having this boy. Still, my husband never came to the hospital, and I wondered why. I returned to my father's house and spent twenty days healing there, getting better. Then my husband and my mother-in-law came to pick me up, and I knew instantly that nothing had changed. Nothing. My husband looked at the baby and said, "Huh. Okay." He shrugged his shoulders. He never kissed our son. He never held him. Nothing.

I soon realized the only reason they had taken me home was because they missed having a maid in the house. That was all. It was the same as the past, except now I had a baby who cried at night and made my husband even angrier than before. Not that my husband ever slept in the room with me. But any sound in the house at night, any crying or fussing, sent him into a rage.

I decided I would get a job in order to support my son and also as a way of getting out of the house. I asked my husband what he thought.

"Whatever," he said. "Just get out if you want to. I don't want to see you."

So I started my new job as a photographer. I tried for my photographer's license, and I was the only woman in a class of 220. I wanted to prove to them that I could do it. But by then, even my father questioned my decision.

"I have money," he complained. "You have a son at home. Why do you work?"

"I can do it," I said. "Just watch."

Soon after I started to make my way in the photography business, my mom called me one night. She said my uncle was there, an uncle I had always loved. When I arrived, he was so excited to see me, even though I was angry at life and proud of the money I was making.

"Ah, Nasrin," he said, smiling. "Tell me the story of your life."

He was so happy. I couldn't understand how someone could have such joy in their heart.

"There is nothing to tell," I said, finally opening up to him. "I am alone. I am sad. My life is terrible."

"I have to tell you something," he said after a long time. "God loves you so much. You're not alone. God even gave His Son for you."

Our time together went from serious to humorous. I couldn't help but laugh.

"What? Did God get married? How could He have a son?" In Islam, if you say that God had a son, then you'd have to also say that God was married, which made no sense.

"Are you crazy?" I asked him. "I don't want to talk anymore."

"So you think I'm so stupid?" he asked.

I nodded, then I laughed again. But he only smiled wider.

One year after that conversation, and after many more fights with my husband and many beatings, I went to Tehran for a class that had to do with photography. While I was there, that same uncle asked if I would go with him to church. I had nothing else to do, so I went. I thought I could go and find something wrong, then point it out to him so that he would stop bothering me about this God who had a son. It sounded ridiculous to me.

When I arrived, everyone was so kind that it completely disarmed me. I was so worried about my hijab and being covered, but no one there seemed concerned about it. My face was so angry, but they didn't mind that either. All the women came and hugged me and told me, "God loves you! Bless you!"

You don't even know me, I thought. *How can you do that? How can you say that to me?*

My cousin gave me a Bible and told me to read John. It would be one of the most important events in my life, receiving that Bible and then reading through the book of John. The language seemed close to Persian in its rhythm and the way it read, and I felt so connected to it. Then I read John 3:16: "For God so loved the world that he gave his one and only Son, that whoever believes in him shall not perish but have eternal life."

I read it again. I thought of my own son. I wondered what it would be like to give him up. I felt something change inside of me, something important, but I didn't know what it was.

Six months later I was in Tehran again for another class. I told my uncle I wanted to go with him to church.

"You don't need an invite?" he asked in mock astonishment.

I don't know why I went. To be prayed for? To be respected? To be loved? I had a great job and, by then, my own photography shop and a beautiful baby boy. But I didn't have myself. My soul was empty.

At church that week they sang a song that included the words, "God loves you and gave you His Son." What was happening to me? Why did I feel the way I felt?

Can you see me, God? Can you help me?

Then, somewhere deep inside of me, close to where those questions came from, I sensed a voice speaking into my empty spaces.

I made you.

I am with you.

I love you.

LIVE | DEAD CHALLENGE

After speaking to nearly fifty Iranian Christians from various parts of the world, I discovered a few common threads are visible in all of their stories. One of these threads is that they were brought to Jesus after first seeing His love displayed among church people. That love, so evident, spilled over onto them, so that they couldn't spend time with believers without also feeling a deep sense of acceptance and love.

We see this throughout Acts, the care that new Believers gave to one another. They didn't put their own lives first but instead sought to heal the wounds of those in their company.

How do we, members of the church in the United States, bear witness to this tradition of love? Are we one in Christ? Do we come around each other and build each other up? Do we look for ways to direct our love to the other parts of the body located around the world?

Spend time thinking and praying for the Iranian church today, that they would continue to show this supernatural love to each other, and that by way of osmosis this love would filter out into their communities, transforming the hearts of their neighbors.

Then, act on these prayers. Fulfill an act of love to one person in your own faith community. Tell someone about Iran and introduce that person to the plight of this strategic nation that, for the most part, has no access to the gospel.

ther. My
spend th
I was bon
Islam. I
hope. Who can I talk to?
paradise? I can never please
no job. I would like to marry and
any of my peers use drugs to escape hopelessness. I read
at will happen to me if I change religions? Someti
become of my family? I am afraid. I feel sad
I live in fear. On the Internet I see othe
on is common. The love of Jesus
of my friends have A
by the C

Nasrin

(PART FOUR)

THE THREE WORDS

On the Sabbath we went outside the city gate to the river, where
we expected to find a place of prayer. We sat down and began to
speak to the women who had gathered there. One of those listening
was a woman from the city of Thyatira named Lydia, a dealer in
purple cloth. She was a worshiper of God. The Lord opened her
heart to respond to Paul's message.

ACTS 16:13–14

I cried there in the church and asked God to help me with my bad situations, my difficult life. Things changed inside of me. I felt my heart begin to soften. My words didn't contain so much hate.

After I came to Christ, I stopped fighting with my husband. He continued to beat me and shout at me, but I couldn't fight back with him anymore. He could tell that I had changed, that I was free. Every morning when I woke up I put on a little bit of makeup, and I didn't cover myself all the time.

"What's wrong with you?" he asked. "Why have you changed? Why won't you fight with me anymore?"

But I didn't say anything.

Then came the time my mother-in-law and I stood in the kitchen together. She turned towards me and spoke in a calm voice full of disgust.

"I hate you," she said. "I would kill you if it didn't mean I'd have to go to prison."

I put my hand on her shoulder. I felt so much pity for her, that she wasn't free.

"Mom," I said (I had never called her that before), "I don't know why you hate me, but I love you."

My husband was behind me and when I said those words he grabbed me and slammed the left side of my head up against the wall. I collapsed to the ground.

"You are a prostitute!" he screamed. "Something is wrong with you!"

I laid on the floor, and the two of them walked out.

I went to the doctor after that incident because I lost hearing in my left ear. My father paid for the surgery to repair my damaged ear, and the doctor said I could expect to regain only 50 percent of my hearing. Even with a damaged ear, I continued to hear that loving voice in my heart.

I made you. I am with you. I love you.

Finally, I took my son and planned to leave, but my husband saw me and beat me. I tried to run because he was so angry. He grabbed a knife and cut me. I tried to run because he was so angry. He grabbed a knife and cut me. I grabbed for the knife, but it went through my hand and sliced along the top of my chest. There was so much blood, and the cut was so deep, just above my heart. I just stood there staring at my hands. Blood was everywhere, pulsing out of me. What was I supposed to do?

They took my son and locked me in my room for three days with no doctor because they were scared of what would happen. They didn't want to get in trouble for what they had done. I lay there in bed and looked down at the blood and the wound. I thought I would die there in that room. I was ready to die.

But my brother-in-law worked with the government and heard about what had happened. He came by and told my husband that he had to take me to a hospital.

"What if she dies here in your house?" he said. "Then what will you do?"

So my husband took me to my father's house because he didn't want to pay for a hospital. My father was shocked. Something switched inside of him. He no longer cared about the shame of a divorce, because he finally recognized how bad it really was. He took me to the hospital, and I had surgeries on my hand and my chest. I still have terrible scars there, long, shiny patches of skin that remind me of that day. They remind me of my past.

After I healed, I went away to Tehran. I didn't have anything anymore: my husband kept my son, my job was finished, my extended family was ashamed of me because of my divorce and because I was a Christian. But I had Jesus. So I joined my uncle in Tehran and went to church and learned more about God. Every time I went to class the women hugged me and I thought, *Wow, Nasrin, you have a great big God.*

Not long after that, I received a call from my mother-in-law. She said that she knew I was a Christian and that she would report me to the government. She said it wasn't anything personal. It was just about Muslims and Christians, and she didn't think that someone who converted to Christianity should live. I didn't say a word the entire time. I just listened. Three days later I left my country.

I arrived in the United States, and I thought to myself, *I have no house? That's okay. I have no son? That's okay. I have only $150? That's okay . . . because I have Jesus.*

I think back on my time in Iran, and I am not filled with anger and hatred because I see that it was one long path that led me to Christ. When I stand in front of a mirror and I touch the long scars on my body, when I hear the ringing in my ears from my damaged ear, I don't feel hate anymore, because I know that Jesus experienced much worse for me.

I simply touch those scars, think of those who have hurt me, and say three words: "I forgive you."

LIVE | DEAD CHALLENGE

In Acts 16 we read that Paul and his disciples looked for a place of prayer outside the city gates. It was the Sabbath, so understandably they looked for a quiet place where they could pray.

Instead, they found a group of women. Among these women was Lydia, a "worshiper of God."

There are many worshipers of God in Iran. Many of the people I met began their story by saying, "When I lived in Iran, I knew there was a God. I loved God. But I felt like there was something more to knowing God than what Islam had to offer."

There are many worshipers of God who need someone to come to them and share the message, just as Nasrin needed her uncle to welcome her into his life and his church.

Today's challenge is simply a series of questions for you to ponder.

Will you leave the city gates behind, will you go outside of your safe space, and seek God through prayer?

Will you listen to the people you encounter when you leave your safe space?

Will you share the message of God's love?

There are many "worshipers of God" in the United States and around the world who still need to hear the message of Jesus Christ, but Live Dead is specifically concerned with the 40 percent of people in the world who have no personal access to the witness of Believers.

Will you help others, through prayer and financial support, take his message to those who have never heard the name of Jesus?

Will you personally take His message to Iran?

I am In
sisters.
as been
h my
crushed
long for
into pain
t no job
Allah, I have
children one day. Many of my
have seems joyful. What will happen
praying to Jesus. What will become of my fan
country is beautiful. I live in fear. On the
Heroin addiction is common. The love of Jes
A number of my friends have All
fascinated by the cross
see

DAY SEVENTEEN

Yasmin

THE QUESTION

---

*But other Jews were jealous; so they rounded up some bad
characters from the marketplace, formed a mob and started a riot
in the city. They rushed to Jason's house in search of Paul and
Silas in order to bring them out to the crowd.*

ACTS 17:5

Seven years after my husband was arrested and imprisoned by
the Iranian authorities, we decided that we had to leave Iran.
Pastors that we knew had been killed. Others were in prison.
Churches were being shut down. For years we had been followed
and our phone lines had been tapped. It felt like we were too
well-known by the authorities to do church work without
endangering those connected to us.

We bought airplane tickets to Turkey, and we counted
down the days until our departure. Some friends drove us to the
airport, but during this entire time I don't think my husband or
I expected the Iranian government would allow us to leave. We

thought that at any moment someone would recognize us and take our passports. Perhaps they had followed us to the airport. Perhaps we had accidentally mentioned something about the trip on our phone, and they had listened in. We didn't know.

We approached passport control, and I was very nervous. The children could sense our uncertainty. Our youngest child still remembers the anxiety of that day, even though it happened over twenty years ago and she was only five or six. We waited in line, and eventually we approached the agent, me and the children first, with my husband to follow. Behind the agent, on a large poster, were the words, "If you have spent even one day in jail, you must tell passport control."

I stepped up to the counter.

"Have you ever spent time in prison?" the agent asked me.

"No," I said. I got even more nervous. Would they ask my husband the same question? What would he say if they did? I couldn't imagine that he would lie about it, even if it was the difference between freedom or staying in Iran. The agent let my children and me pass through.

I didn't have to wait long before my husband joined us.

"What did you say when they asked if you had ever been in prison?" I asked my husband.

"They never asked me," he said, shrugging his shoulders and smiling.

We saw God's hand, that day and many other days. How beautifully He protected us and erased our past from the eyes of the passport agents. We easily got out of the country, a miracle from God. Now we are here, in the United States. My husband passed away not long ago, but my children and I continue to serve God in this country.

LIVE | DEAD CHALLENGE

Imagine living where you are constantly watched and pursued by those who would like to put you in prison and throw away the key. Imagine, every time you go to church, you have to look up and down the street before you leave your house to make sure you are not being watched or followed. Imagine thinking twice about saying the name Jesus during a phone call for fear that your phone is tapped.

There is a dependency and trust in God that forms only in a space of volatility and uncertainty, when you don't know what will happen tomorrow, and you have to believe completely that God will make a path for you.

Here is a dangerous prayer to pray, but if you are committed to living dead, then it's a prayer you must become comfortable with.

"Father God, I am willing to go where you want me to go, to be what you want me to be, to endure what you would have me endure. Please use me for to further your kingdom as you see fit. Put clear paths in front of me so that I will know how you want me to serve. Amen."

Write this prayer down and pray it throughout the day and the rest of the time you spend reading this book. Then, when a path clears in front of you, follow it.

the
born a
to live
can I
can ne
ld. like

Me
holiday. I a
Muslim. I a
spiritual poverty. I a
peers use
will God. allow me into
I have a degree but no job
children one day. Many of my peers use
Allah.
happen to me ?
of my family?
Jesus. What will become
seems joyful. What will happen to me ?
beautiful. I live in fear. On the I
addiction is common. The
number of my friends
by the cross.
escorted

Zahra

THE UNDERGROUND

One night the Lord spoke to Paul in a vision: "Do not be afraid;
keep on speaking, do not be silent. For I am with you, and no
one is going to attack and harm you, because I have many people
in this city." So Paul stayed in Corinth for a year and a half,
teaching them the word of God.

ACTS 18:9–11

I was five years old when my father died, but I have many memories of him. He was the kind of man who came home from work and played with me and my sister and brother. Before bed, he told us stories. He was such a good father.

He was also a devout Muslim, and I grew up as any girl with a wonderful, devout Muslim father would grow up. I watched my father say his prayers, and I wanted to say prayers. I heard the calls to prayer, and they filled me with a sense of holiness and longing for God.

Because of my family's strict adherence to Islam, it was easy to understand why they treated my Christian uncle so poorly. Eventually he moved to Tehran to start a new life, but when he came back to our home town, our family forced him to eat from separate dishes so we would not be defiled.

My father became extremely sick and died. For many years after he died, I struggled with God over his death. Why would God allow this to happen? I didn't hear any answers, but my Christian uncle moved back to our city so he could help my mother care and provide for us, her three children.

My mother became close to my uncle, and his way of life began to influence her. She explored Christianity but was terrified that God would be angry with her. She was scared that if she converted to Christianity she would go to hell when she died. So she continued praying her Muslim prayers even as she learned more and more about Christ.

She did both for a while, but soon a lady from my uncle's church asked if she could disciple her. My mother went to that lady's house, and as soon as she arrived she realized she had been to this place before and had met with this woman before—*in a dream!* The lady taught my mother, and after a while my mother gave her heart to the Lord.

My brother was fifteen years old when my mother became a Christian, and he called her names because of her new faith. He was so antagonistic towards her and my uncle. He called them unclean and those sorts of things, but there was also something in him that began to change, something that was moved by my uncle's love.

One night, he and my sister traveled on an overnight bus ride. Neither of the two had confessed faith in Christ up to that point. It was a long night, dark and quiet. Most of the people on the bus were asleep. Suddenly, out of nowhere, my brother and sister turned to each other and said the same thing simultaneously.

"Do you want to follow Jesus?"

Something had come over them in that instant, something unexpected and beautiful, and from that time on our entire family followed after God. Our church grew to ten families. We met in our homes, but at that time we were not particularly fearful of what the government would do to us. We thought we were willing to pay any price.

I arrived home from school one day when I was fourteen. My sister met me at the door, her face covered in tears. She could barely speak.

"Zahra, do you know what happened?" she asked.

"No," I said, coming inside, a sense of panic filling me.

"Pastor was killed today," she said, crying fresh tears.

I cried every night for a long, long time. After that, our church consisted of only a few families. We became much more careful. Sometimes our church was just our family, sitting in our living room. One of us played the piano, another led worship, and then my uncle would preach or we would listen to a Christian tape.

As I got more and more involved in the underground church, I had to become increasingly cautious. Sometimes, before a church service, I would go shopping and run many errands just to make sure no one was following me to where our church was meeting on that particular day. Sometimes I spent the night at a friend's house.

For Christmas or other Christian celebrations, we would tell the parishioners to be ready on a particular day, but no one besides the leaders knew the time or the place. So the parishioners would wait all day until we pulled up outside their house, and then they'd quickly get in the car and we'd whisk them off to wherever we were gathering.

Those were difficult times, but they were also great times because we could sense the Holy Spirit so clearly, and God's cover was over us. They were hard experiences, but they were also great experiences.

LIVE | DEAD CHALLENGE

"Do not be afraid," God told Paul. "Keep on speaking."

Fear is a real obstacle for believers in Iran, and fear is what their enemies use to control them.

While few of us in the United States have to fear death or imprisonment because of our faith, our enemy, the same one those in Iran face, still uses fear to keep us from serving God, speaking about God, and living out God's destiny for our lives.

What is the one thing God is calling you to do today?

What is the fear or list of fears that keeps you from moving down the path God has prepared for you?

Today, God is telling you: "Do not be afraid."

Today, God is saying: "Do not be silent."

Would you ask God how you can Live Dead so that those without access to the gospel can hear it?

and one brother have

ther has been sick I

...ys with my cousins. I

I am crushed by Is...

...rty. I long for hope. W...

...w me into paradise. I

...egree but no job. I

...Man...

...se

...to

I feel sad...

"When we seek to do God's will, we find ourselves in the midst of God's bigger story and playing a part in God's redemptive work in other people's lives."

ADAM HAMILTON

Iranian ... and on
... been sick
holidays with my cousins
Muslim. I am crushed by Isl...
spiritual poverty. I long for hope. Wha...
Will God allow me into paradise? I can...
Allah. I have a degree but no job. I could like to...
have children one day. Many of my peers use drugs...
... seems joyful. What will happen to me if I...
... to Jesus. What will become of my family?
... is beautiful. I live in fear. On the Ir...
... addiction is common. The...
... nber of my frie...

Ashur

THE UPPER ROOM

Paul entered the synagogue and spoke boldly there for three months, arguing persuasively about the kingdom of God. But some of them became obstinate; they refused to believe and publicly maligned the Way. So Paul left them.

ACTS 19:8–9

After the revolution, it seemed like all the jobs were gone. My brother-in-law, Ashur, had worked for an international company, but once the Islamic Revolution took place, most foreign companies left Iran and many people suddenly had no employment. So Ashur and his wife, my sister Mahin, moved in with us.

Ashur loved Jesus. He diligently looked for a job, but his heart beat to serve the Lord. Every time he knelt in the presence of God, he cried like a child. As the months passed, he decided he would stop looking for work and simply serve God, go where he was called, and spread the gospel.

An Assyrian Pentecostal church sent him and his wife to a small city that had an old, nearly abandoned church. It was a cold place, and in the summer scorpions lived in the dust. But Ashur and Mahin went there eager to share the Word of God.

They had their second child in that city, so with their young family they began to plant a church. There were few Assyrians there, so Ashur worked with the Kurdish people as well. It was a friendly community. They welcomed Ashur and his family.

There was an admissions office in Tehran that people would contact if they were interested in Christianity, and this office sent Ashur all of the contact information for people from his new city who had reached out to that office. He planned a church service and invited everyone from that list—they were all Iranian or Kurdish, which meant that few of them understood Assyrian. From that moment, he began to preach the Word of God in Farsi, and it was very successful. This was in 1986 or 1987, when the government didn't want anyone to preach about Jesus in Farsi.

Ashur tried other ways to grow the church. He took tracts or brochures everywhere he went—these had the church's information on the back. No one had cell phones in those days, so everything he did was by word of mouth, handing out pamphlets in shopping malls or markets, and talking with anyone willing to chat. Since he was new to the city, he often spent entire days wandering the streets, handing out brochures to anyone who would take them.

My husband and I often went and helped him. Sometimes we walked through snow up to our knees. Sometimes the water in Ashur's apartment would freeze, and we had no water to drink or even to wash our faces. He held the church service in this apartment, usually in the smaller upper room because it cost too much to heat the entire building. It was crowded, but God was there.

Ashur and Mahin had their third child. Besides their family and their church, Ashur and my sister had nothing. They survived on practically nothing. Whatever they had, they put the best out for their guests or for the people in their church.

During that time, you couldn't buy whatever you wanted—you had a ration coupon that allowed you to purchase certain things. For one family, for one month, you might have a coupon for a chicken, a certain number of coupons for sugar cubes and milk. If Ashur and his wife had extra coupons, they never used them for themselves. They always gave them to families who had less than they had.

Before my husband and I left Iran, we asked Ashur and my sister to consider leaving Iran as well. It was becoming extremely difficult and dangerous for pastors to live in that country. They were put in prison and persecuted. Churches were shut down. Finally, Ashur agreed to leave.

He and his wife sold the house an old couple had given to them, and they used the money to apply for visas and new passports for themselves and their children. They planned on going to Malaysia and, eventually, the United States.

But when they arrived at the airport, they were not allowed to leave.

"Either you or your wife must stay behind," the Iranian official told Ashur. "The rest of you are free to go."

"We cannot go without each other!" Ashur protested. "We have to be together!"

The official shrugged.

"That is none of my business," he said. "One of you must stay behind."

So they left the airport, and once again they had nothing. No house to return to. No money. Their passports had been stamped so they could never leave the country. They traveled back to their cold city and looked for a place to stay. They ended up back in their original apartment, the one they couldn't afford to heat, the one where the church had met in the upper room.

Yet they continued the work of God in that city. They continued to work with their small church and gave everything they had to those around them.

LIVE | DEAD CHALLENGE

Every day, Christians in Iran face questions. Should they tell their families they are Christians or should they let it remain a secret? Should they invite a new friend to church or will that put everyone else in danger? Should they stay in Iran, or should they try to leave?

There is no single answer that works for every Iranian Christian. So much depends on their particular situation, where they live, and who they are talking to.

Spend time in prayer today for the Christians in Iran, specifically asking that they will receive supernatural guidance to know how to answer these questions.

I am I...

three sisters

Mother has bee[n]

holidays with my

Muslim. I am crushe[d]

...al poverty I long fo[r]

into p...

but no j...

ny of...

ill happ...

of my

fear. On...

mon...

friends have...

of Jesus...

questions are arrested. My

I don't sleep I as thought about

things on the Internet about Jesus. I s...

Pari

THE DRESS CODE

When Paul had finished speaking, he knelt down with all of them and prayed. They all wept as they embraced him and kissed him. What grieved them most was his statement that they would never see his face again. Then they accompanied him to the ship.

ACTS 20:36–38

M y children are too young to remember the way Iran used to be before the revolution. They never experienced the freedom we experienced prior to this regime. My two older children eventually moved to Germany, but my youngest daughter, Pari, remained behind with us and dealt with the struggles of living under the regime.

When Pari turned eighteen, the dress code became extremely strict. She was considered a woman, and it was important that she remain fully covered. She wore a hajib that covered her hair and encircled her face—even with that on, she had to make sure none of her hair was showing around her forehead, and she couldn't wear any makeup.

One day she went to a square in the city to grab a cup of coffee with some of her work friends. In those types of public places there is always a police command post or a checkpoint or something like that. The government wants to remind the citizens of its power and presence. It often feels like the police are everywhere.

Normally, the male police officers deal with men and the female police officers deal with women. This ensures that everyone can stay in line with the laws regarding purity and modesty. But on that particular day, one of the male police officers approached my daughter.

"You need to come forward," he said in a firm voice.

"Me?" Pari asked.

"Yes, you."

She thought about it for a moment, wondering why the officer had called her over. She hadn't done anything wrong, at least not that she was aware of. Instead of stepping toward him, she took a few steps back.

"I'm not going anywhere until you call for my parents," she said. "What have I done wrong that you're calling me over?"

"You're not following the dress code."

She felt up around her face to make sure none of her hair had snuck out from beneath her hijab.

"Why?" she asked. "How have I broken the dress code? I'm wearing clothes and boots. I don't have any makeup on. What have I done wrong?"

"The tops of your boots are showing," the man said in a flat voice. "Your pants should be outside your boots, not inside."

At that point, he instructed the two female police officers to arrest Pari, but she resisted when the women tried to grab her arms. The police keep several vans close to those outposts in case they need to take many people to prison at one time, and they led her toward the row of vans. She continued to resist.

When they tried to pull her into one of the vans, she kicked one of the police officers in the chest, knocking her inside the vehicle. The officer grabbed her radio and called for backup. That's when my daughter started shouting as loudly as she could.

"I haven't done anything wrong!" she screamed. "I haven't done anything wrong!"

A crowd gathered. Her friends and coworkers came over to see what was going on. Pari started crying and hyperventilating, and the crowd became angry at the police.

"What's the problem here?" one of the male police officers asked as he came over.

The crowd began to argue with him.

"She hasn't done anything wrong!" they insisted. "If this girl has a heart attack right now, how will you explain that?"

Meanwhile, my daughter grabbed on to a small tree and wouldn't let go. At first the police tried to pry her from the tree, but soon the crowd moved in, surrounded her, and forced the police back. The crowd distracted the police while some of Pari's friends went and got a car. They drove her away before the police knew what had happened.

These are the kinds of things that happen in Iran every day. You never know when you might do something little that will draw the attention of the police. It is even worse if you are a Christian. It becomes almost impossible to meet all of the legal requirements, and even when you do, they make something up in order to arrest you.

I wish we could experience freedom in Iran.

LIVE | DEAD CHALLENGE

The second half of Acts is filled with good-byes as Jesus' disciples began to travel out from Jerusalem. They made new friends as they journeyed, but then they had to travel on to other places. Some of the farewells were "see you later," when they hoped their paths would cross again. Others were "good-bye," when they knew they were about to be arrested.

Today, there are people who have said good-bye to family and friends and have moved to the Middle East to spread the gospel in and around Iran. Like the worker who wrote the preface to this book, those who choose to go say good-bye to friends and family. They hope to cross paths with them again, but whenever you go to a part of the world that is hostile to Christians and to the gospel, you never know when that next meeting might be.

Is the love of friends and family the only thing that keeps you from taking the gospel to people who have never heard? Is saying good-bye the one thing you are trying not to do?

If that's the case, ask God to fill you with an overwhelming desire to go, a desire that would be stronger than your hesitancy to say good-bye.

If you don't feel called to go to Iran, spend time today praying for those who do. Pray that there will be no hesitancy, but that they will lean into the next step, and the next step, and the next step. Pray that saying good-bye will not keep them from going.

Shapur

THE SHORT VACATION

*Then Paul answered, "Why are you weeping and breaking
my heart? I am ready not only to be bound, but also to die in
Jerusalem for the name of the Lord Jesus." When he would not be
dissuaded, we gave up and said, "The Lord's will be done."*

ACTS 21:13–14

After Pastor Haik Hovsepian was killed in January of 1994, the government began to put a lot of pressure on the pastors in Iran. There was a palpable fear in those days, but there were also many pastors who refused to allow the martyrdom of Pastor Hovsepian to deter them from spreading the gospel. In return, the government created new guidelines for pastors. They had to report where they were going, who they met with, their reasons for travel, and when they would return from their destinations.

Remember my brother-in-law, Ashur (Chapter Nineteen)? The one we had finally convinced to leave Iran, only for he and his family to be turned away at the airport? Years passed, and when he was around forty years old, we watched from outside the country as the circle around him grew tighter and tighter. Whenever he left the city to visit relatives or to encourage other churches, he had to report everything. As time passed, he became frustrated, and I think sometimes he just wanted to go somewhere without telling everyone. The work of God needed to continue, even if they denied his requests.

In the meantime, Ashur and his wife were like parents to many of the young men and women who had left Islam and become Christians, because many of their families no longer accepted them. In many cases, Ashur was able to talk to their families and bring about reconciliation for them. He was doing a great work.

The government began to request that he report at random times and answer questions, but he managed to stay vague in his responses, and the police, for whatever reason, didn't press for details. So for a time he got away with general answers, but they had spies in the church. Perhaps that's why they didn't press him for information—they already had it. They questioned him about events or people they couldn't have known about without information from inside the church.

My husband and I and our two children left Iran, and the moment we left, they took Ashur into custody. Apparently he had signed something that said he would never leave the city again without permission, but there were seminars and conferences for Christians in other areas of Iran where he was needed, so he had traveled without seeking their permission. He was arrested on his way to another city.

Ashur spent almost three months in prison, and when he was finally allowed to leave, he wasn't well . . . physically or emotionally.

He was extremely afraid, not of what they would do to him, but of what they would do to his wife or children. He wanted to leave Iran, but he and his wife bided their time and waited.

About a year after his imprisonment, they boarded a bus and made it look like they were taking a short vacation to Turkey. They took only a few small bags and left their house and all of their other belongings behind. We didn't even know they were going to leave because they didn't want to risk anyone hearing their plan.

There are certain parts of Iran where it is easy to cross into Turkey, places where the border is not guarded as closely as others. It was still a huge risk, but they took it. The bus drove slowly over the mountains, and somehow they made it out. God was shielding them, protecting them.

We have never asked the exact route they took, because those routes might still be used by other Christians who need to leave. We don't want to share that information, and we pray that, someday, the routes will be open the other way, so that Christians can go freely into Iran and share the good news of the gospel with those who are under the heel of oppression.

Now Ashur lives in the States with his family and continues to preach the gospel to the Persians who have found their way here.

LIVE | DEAD CHALLENGE

Sometimes those around us find it hard to accept God's call on our lives, especially when it leads to difficulties or a life that is different from the one everyone expects us to live. This criticism and doubt comes from a place of love, because our loved ones want to see us do well. They want to see us thrive.

But it is difficult when your family cannot support the mission God calls you to embark upon. It can be difficult when friends see your acts of faith as irresponsible or imprudent.

Do you feel that those close to you support you when you make difficult decisions about following Christ, or do they misunderstand?

Pray for those who have an unconventional call on their lives, perhaps to take the gospel to difficult places that most people deem "unsafe." Pray that their friends and family would be supportive of this call, and that in those cases where support is not felt, those individuals would receive the strength and peace they need to obey the call of God.

I am Iranian...
...sisters and...
...has been...
...ps with my a...
I am crushed by...
al poverty. I long for hope. Who can I talk to?
...God. I have a degree but no job. I can never please...
allow me into paradise? I can never marry and
...children one day. Many of my peers use drugs to escape...
is joyful. What will happen to me if I change religions? Hopelessness. I
...well become of my family? I am afraid. I feel...
...d. I live in fear. On the Internet I see of...
...tion is common. The love of Jes...
...of my friends have...
...d by the...

Ehsan

THE MARRIAGE

> *"You will be his witness to all people of what you have seen and heard. And now what are you waiting for? Get up, be baptized and wash your sins away, calling on his name."*
>
> ACTS 22:15–16

My marriage to my wife, Banu, was an arranged marriage. My grandmother was Banu's cousin's neighbor (if you can follow that, you're doing well!). So my family, and especially my mother and aunt, would often visit at her cousin's house. Also, my sister was friends with her sister, and I remembered seeing Banu from time to time when we were growing up. She didn't remember me, but that didn't keep me from having my mom call her parents and tell them that we'd like to come and ask for their daughter's hand in marriage.

After the proposal came the request for permission to get engaged. This begins with an official gathering when the groom's family meets with the bride's family. It is sort of like a proposal except the entire family does the asking. Then the bride can decide if she wants to marry or not, and even the groom can change his mind. During that gathering, the families discuss the dowry and wedding details. Sometimes, even if the bride and groom want to get married, these details cannot be agreed on and the whole thing is called off.

I had seen Banu ten years before, and after the gathering she said she liked me but she would also like to get to know me better, just to see if our personalities matched and if we had things in common. We dated. We went to restaurants and the theatre.

We dated for eighteen months before the wedding. When we first got married, she was studying physics at the university, and after she graduated I insisted that we leave Iran. I had grown weary of the changing government and how little freedom there was in the country. I hired an attorney to help us with our business affairs and visa issues. It took us four years to prepare everything.

I was not sad to leave Iran, but my wife depended on her family quite a bit, and she loved them, so it was hard for her to say good-bye. In Iran I worked in a machine shop. I had seventeen years of experience in that profession, and I worked with the military and other large corporations.

But when I arrived in the United States, the only job I could get was at a gas station. I ran the register and stocked shelves and helped people when they had problems with the filling station or the bathroom. Soon my wife worked there as well, and it was hard for me to watch my wife, my beautiful wife, empty the trash cans and clean the bathroom.

But I wasn't discouraged because I had a goal. We had come to stay. Soon I had three jobs: working at the gas station, packaging makeup and cosmetics, and a third part-time job.

That's when we started to attend a church, after a friend invited us to listen to a music solo. In the beginning, my wife's faith grew strong, but I wasn't so sure. She insisted on being in church every Sunday, but I didn't care one way or the other.

Then I heard a sermon that changed my heart, and suddenly I wanted to be a soldier for God. I was attracted to the church, and I felt like it was *my* church . . . *my* religion. From that day on I wanted to serve people—it didn't matter what they needed. I just wanted to serve. So I cleaned the church, I sang up front, and sometimes I made mistakes but my brothers and sisters in Christ never made fun of me. They were so encouraging.

My wife and I were baptized in 2010, and it was such a beautiful experience, surrounded by our friends, those who had become family to us. We continue to serve at the church God gave to us, and life is so good.

My wife went back to Tehran for a month not too long ago. While she was there, we both worried because her family is a strict Muslim family, and we thought that if they found out she was a Christian they might not let her return to the States. But God gave us peace, and she had a safe trip.

Now we are expecting our first child, after many, many years of not being able to conceive. It is just another blessing that God has given us, and we look forward to what the future holds.

LIVE | DEAD CHALLENGE

What a powerful section of Acts, when Paul retold the story of his conversion. My favorite part is when Paul told what God said to him, and there's one question that God asked that stands out.

"And now, what are you waiting for?" (Acts 22:2)

It's a good question to ask ourselves from time to time.

"And now, what am I waiting for?"

Am I waiting for perfect conditions? Am I waiting for someone else to change? Am I waiting for a sign?

In this passage, God followed up the question, "And now, what are you waiting for?" with a command to go and be baptized. If God were speaking directly to you today, what command would follow the question?

And now, what are you waiting for? Go and . . .

r. My
pend the
was born
Islam. I live in
pe Who can I talk to
rade? I can never please
o job I would like to marry and
of my peers use drugs to escape hopelessness. I read someth
appen to me if I change religions? Sometimes I
to me if I change religions? Sometimes I
n fear. On the Internet I see others
will become of my family? I am afraid I feel sad Christ
addiction is common. The love of Jesus is very
n fear. On the Internet I see others
I live in fear. On the Internet I see others
mber of my friends have AIDS I
itful I live in fear. On the Internet I see others
by the Cross
the Cross

Sara

THE FAST

The following night the LORD stood near Paul and
said, "Take courage! As you have testified about me
in Jerusalem, so you must also testify in Rome."

ACTS 23:11

I remember how my husband and I were usually the first people at church, and how some mornings we would find folded scraps of paper in the courtyard that someone had thrown over the wall. My husband would pick the paper up, unfold it, and read it.

"If you don't stop having church here, we are going to burn the place down."

That was all that was written. There was no name . . . nothing else. My husband and I never told anyone in the congregation; we simply prayed harder for God to intervene in our city and to protect the church from those who would harm it. Then we burned the piece of paper and prepared the church for the service that day.

One of our friends worked hard with my husband to spread the good news throughout our city. Soon, more and more people came to church. It became clear that our duty was to proclaim the gospel to the Muslims in the city, so that's what we started to do. This meant we had to preach in Farsi, which was illegal but extremely important as it helped the Muslim people who came to the church understand what we were talking about.

The church was still rather small, but more people came all the time. It was a close-knit group of people who loved each other with all their hearts. We were like brothers and sisters, which was good because many had lost their families when they became Christians. We shared what little we had. We paid each other's bills. We ate meals together, and we always served the best food, even if it was all we had.

Then my husband felt impressed to fast for the spiritual awakening of Iran, not just our city but for the entire country. He prayed that the communist rule would pass from every country around us. Mostly he prayed that the eyes of the Iranian people would be opened to the truth. Humbly I say this: he drank only water for forty-five days. His weight dropped from 165 pounds to fifty-five pounds. Gradually, he started to lose his memory. His bones pushed out against his skin. He rarely got out of bed.

Finally, at the end of forty-five days, he decided to end his fast, and three days later he became extremely ill. We took him to the hospital, where the doctors told us that because of his extended fast, his blood was no longer providing sufficient nutrients to his brain. They took care of him there, and after a week or so we brought him home. But his brain activity had diminished, and he was weak. We had some difficult days after that.

Twice the doctors admitted him to the intensive care unit in Tehran, and his condition was so serious that no one was allowed to visit him. This time he came home with all kinds of medications, so many different pills and bottles and instructions. But with faith in the blood of Jesus, after one year he no longer needed to take any medicine.

We knew that God had extended His hand and healed him. My husband became extremely healthy, and even his memory came back to him.

If we want God's truth to become known to Iran, we must be willing to do anything He asks us to do . . . anything.

LIVE | DEAD CHALLENGE

It required immense courage to be part of the early church in the years following the crucifixion and resurrection of Jesus. Every time Paul or one of his disciples went to the synagogue, every time they spoke publicly about the gospel, every time they healed someone or performed a miracle, they ran the risk of imprisonment or stoning.

That's why Acts 23 is so important.

"Take courage!" the Lord told Paul.

Why should Paul take courage? Did God promise that nothing bad would happen to him? Did God promise a "hedge of protection"? Did God guarantee that all of Paul's enemies would be vanquished?

No.

"Take courage! As you have testified about me in Jerusalem, so you must also testify in Rome" (Acts 23:11.)

In other words, God encouraged Paul to stay strong and brave because God had a purpose for Paul's life and there was still work for him to do.

What is your purpose? Knowing God's purpose for your life increases your ability to remain courageous even in the most difficult circumstances. David had the courage to face Goliath, in part because David knew he would one day be king of Israel.

Pray today that God would show you clearly His purpose for your life. Pray that our Iranian brothers and sisters would know God's purpose for their lives and that this would lead them to a place of courage.

I am I
three sisters
Mother has been
holidays with my
Muslim. I am crushed
spiritual poverty I long for
Will God allow me into par...
...e a degree but no job
...y of my
...happen
...my fam
...on. The Internet I
...on. The love of Jes
...ed Christians are
...something on the Internet about Jes...
...not live
...sometimes I...I se thought

DAY TWENTY-FOUR

Fatemah

THE JUDGE

Several days later Felix came with his wife Drusilla,
who was Jewish. He sent for Paul and listened to
him as he spoke about faith in Christ Jesus.

ACTS 24:24

Two years ago, the Iranian government took my mother's passport when she was at the airport on her way to visit us in Turkey. Her name is Fatemah. After that, the government officials were extremely unkind to her, both at the airport and later at the courthouse. Even though she was an older woman and did everything to follow the rules, they disrespected her and made fun of her for being a Christian.

Soon after that my father became ill and died. My mother mourned his passing, and one day while she was going through his things she found his prayer journal. One of his prayers stood out to her: "Please, dear God, don't only have the Iranian government return my wife's passport, but have them deliver it to her front door."

After my dad died, my mom was more desperate to visit us, so she went to the courthouse almost every week, every month, trying to get her passport. One day while she was there they made so much fun of her that she started to cry. Her heart was broken after so many years of difficulties. She felt discouraged and wanted to go home, but something directed her to speak to the head of the court.

Mom was so broken that she cried and cried. When she finally gained an audience with the judge, she was nervous that he would be a mullah and would make fun of her and kick her out. But he wasn't. He was kind to her.

"Please have a seat, Fatemah," he said in a quiet voice, and then he turned to one of his assistants. "Could you please bring this woman some water to drink?"

This definitely wasn't normal. It caught my mother off guard. Then he turned and spoke with her.

"Okay," he said. "Can you tell me your story?"

Because he was kind, my mom started to cry and cry. She didn't know where to begin.

"Please, Fatemah," he said again, "tell me your story. I'd like to hear about your life and what has brought you here."

So she told him everything that had happened. How our pastor had been killed for his faith and how our church was no longer able to meet together. She told him all about our family— all the difficulties . . . all the suffering.

He looked at her, studied her for a moment.

"Are you telling me the truth?" he asked.

"Yes!" she insisted. "Yes. You can go and interview these people. Check the Internet. It's all there."

"Okay," he said, "would you write all this down for me?"

She wrote everything down. It took her quite some time. When she finished, she handed it to him, and he stepped closer to her.

"Can I kiss your gray hair?" he asked. This is a sign of deep respect for our elders, and for him to do this seemed strange to my mother, coming from him, a government worker, a judge. He asked her more questions while she wrote her story; he even skipped the Muslim call to prayer while my mother was with him. After she finished writing her story, he told her to come back in a few weeks.

When she returned, he sat across from her again.

"I took your story home," he said, "and I read it with my wife. Both of us started to cry for you."

My mother was so thankful to have someone finally show her respect, to show her love. It was so abnormal for this to happen to Christians when dealing with the government, and my mom barely knew how to act around this kind man.

"Here's a letter for you to take to another government office."

My mother opened it and couldn't believe her eyes. In the letter, the judge insisted that they return her passport! After she delivered the letter, she returned home, but she didn't have long to wait before the government returned her passport. They delivered it to her front door, just as my father had prayed would happen.

LIVE | DEAD CHALLENGE

In Acts 24 we glimpse how Paul's persecution led him higher and higher up the ranks of government officials. One official came to him, and he shared the gospel, only to be transferred to the next highest ranking official. In this way, he shared the hope of Christ in places it might never have reached.

We see this in Fatemah's story as well. Her testimony was scorned by clerks in the local government office, but when she spoke to a higher judge he listened to her and heard about her hope in Christ.

Could it be that the temporary afflictions we face are simply precursors to a more crucial mission? Could it be that, if we remain patient, God will use us to take His message to people who would never have heard it otherwise?

Pray today that God would give Christians in Iran opportunities to share their faith with those in positions of authority. Pray that they would be bold in sharing their powerful personal testimonies.

Ask God again how you can join the cause to spread the gospel to Iran.

have
ne brother.
ick. I spe
ousins. I was born a
ed by Islam. I live in
s for hope. Who can I talk to?
into paradise? I can never please
but no job I would like to marry and
Many of my peers use drugs to escape hopelessness.
What will happen to me if I change religions? I
will become of my family? I am afraid I fee
I live in fear. On the Internet I see
is common. The love of
my friends ha
by t

Shireen

THE FIVE-HOUR JAIL TERM

*Instead, they had some points of dispute with him
about their own religion and about a dead man
named Jesus who Paul claimed was alive.*

ACTS 25:19

When I was a child, I didn't think about things like freedom. But as I grew older I started to realize how confined people could feel, how controlled. Then things started happening to me—these were no longer just stories I heard about but things I experienced firsthand. Life becomes difficult when you realize this is not going to be an easy place to live, yet it is still your country.

When I was fifteen years old, I spent the mornings at home by myself. My parents were already at work, and I got ready to go to school. A friend of mine who had a boyfriend asked if they could meet at my house—they weren't allowed to hang out in public because they would be punished or arrested or at least given a hard time.

LIVE DEAD: THE STORY

So they came into my house. I laughed and said hello and continued to get ready for school while they hung out in the living room. We were all dressed properly, as if we were outside. Neither my friend nor I wore anything revealing, our hair was covered, everything was as it should have been. My friend and her boyfriend sat on the couch and talked.

"I'm almost ready!" I shouted from the back. That's when I heard a loud knock on the door. By the time I got to the front of the house, the religious police had already entered. Apparently, one of the neighbors reported that a young man had entered a young woman's house.

All of us were around fifteen years old, but they took us to the local jail and put us in with other inmates, mostly thieves, prostitutes, and drug addicts. It was a big room sectioned off into many cells, and there were several women in each cell. I was so scared, not only of what the government would do to me but also what these women might do to me. At that moment I was overwhelmed at the absurdity of the situation.

What did we do to deserve this treatment?

I was in prison for five hours until they called my father and he came to pick me up. At no point did I ever see a judge or learn what I was charged with. At no point did anyone sit down with me and explain anything, although they did say in passing, as my father and I left the jail, that I technically had not done anything wrong and they were simply waiting for my father to come and pick me up.

"If Shireen didn't do anything wrong, why was she taken in the first place?" My father asked.

"She brought a young man into your house, but we know now that she was tricked into doing so," replied the authorities.

"No, I wasn't tricked," I said. "I knew what was going on the whole time. You're just trying to play down what I had done because it's so silly that I'm even here."

They continued to insist I had been tricked, and they let me go.

I returned to school the next day, but there was no sign of my friend. After three days, when she didn't come to school, I called her house. Her sister answered.

"Where is she?" I asked.

"Shireen," my friend's sister whispered, "she's not doing well. The guards beat her horribly."

"What?" I exclaimed. "She's not even fifteen yet, she's a girl. How can they do that?"

"They placed a Koran under their arm and held it against their side, then whipped her while holding the rod in the hand of that arm. That is supposed to limit how hard they can hit a woman, but they gave her fifty lashes. She is in rough shape."

Do you know that we never talked about that incident ever again? We were so embarrassed by what had happened that we never spoke of it to each other. I never even found out what happened to my friend's boyfriend. It was such a humiliating experience.

Soon after that experience I sought out Christianity. I knew a few people who had left Islam, and one of my close friends, a neighbor, started taking me to church with her. Service was Sunday night at 8:00 p.m., and the only way a person could attend was with an existing member—this was a rule to try to keep spies out of the church.

I felt so far from God during that time, and after my experience of going to jail I hated religion, any religion. But there was something about my Christian friends that attracted me. One night I felt sad and depressed, so I went to talk to the friend who had first taken me to church.

She prayed for me that night. I felt a sense of calmness, a sense of peace like I had never felt before, and I fell asleep and slept through the night.

"What prayer did you pray last night?" I asked her.

She taught me more about Christ and salvation, and that's when I became a believer.

LIVE | DEAD CHALLENGE

An argument raged between Paul and the religious authorities: Was Christ alive or dead? Was the Man they had seen on the cross dead and buried or was He, as Paul claimed, risen and alive?

The same question continues today. Did that Nazarene, the one taken down from the cross and put in a tomb, actually rise from the dead after three days? Did He really spend time with His disciples? Did He really rise up and disappear in the clouds?

Perhaps the greatest witness to the resurrection of Jesus Christ is the changed lives of those who follow Him. The same resurrection power that brought Him out of the grave exhibits itself in the transformed lives of those who call on His name.

Have you submitted yourself to the transforming power of Christ? Have you allowed Him to resurrect the dead and dying parts of your life? Many people make a confession of faith but linger in the land of self-reliance, striving to maintain control over their lives and to live a life of predictable outcomes.

In your prayers and your journal today, recommit your life to Christ, not to reassure yourself of your eternal destiny, but to die to your selfish desires and to enter into the exciting plan of resurrected life in Christ.

After you make this commitment, after you submit yourself to His resurrection power, ask if He has called you to share this incredible transformation with the people living in Iran. Journal about how this question makes you feel. Fearful? Angry? Anxious? Excited?

ESTHER'S DAUGHTER

Esther

THE ROOF ENTRANCE

Than Agrippa said to Paul, "Do you think that in such
a short time you can persuade me to be a Christian?"
Paul replied, "Short time or long—I pray to God that
not only you but all who are listening to me today
may become what I am, except for these chains."

ACTS 26:28–29

I lived in my neighborhood for over thirty years and never realized there was a church next door to my house. Sometimes, when my neighbors and I stopped to talk in the street, they asked me about that building.

"Do you think it might be a church?" they asked me.

"No," I always said. "I'm sure it's not."

After many years of wondering, one day I found myself staring at the front door. *I might as well ask them if they are a church,* I thought to myself, so I walked up and knocked. That's when I met the woman who eventually led me to Christ.

But that came later. In the meantime, I was a devout Muslim, and everyone knew that about me. They knew that I always prayed during the calls to prayer. They knew that I had meetings in my house when women would come and we would study the Koran. They knew that I fasted during the appropriate times.

But then I asked about the church. I started attending, secretly and carefully, so that none of my neighbors would see me going in or coming out of that building. I found out that the owner of the building rented it to the leaders for their church. I became a Christian and attended services twice a week, on Sundays and Wednesdays. I loved the people in that church, and I did everything I could to attend each and every service.

It was hard for me as a Christian to have the church next door to my house, because my neighbors were nosey and paid close attention to everyone who went into that building. A few of my friends had converted to Christianity, and we sometimes talked about our faith, but we had to be careful. If anyone found out we were Christians, they would report us.

On Easter morning, our church served a big breakfast and then had a service. My daughter had become a Christian by this time, and we both wanted to attend the Easter service! Celebrating the resurrection of Jesus with our Christian friends was important to us. But every time I looked through the windows at the front of our house, our neighbor was standing at her door watching the people who were going into the church.

If we tried to sneak in, she would see us.

We called a friend who was already in the church and asked him to open the skylight in the roof. So he opened the skylight, and my daughter climbed around from our back deck onto the church roof, and they helped her down into the church. But I was much older than my daughter and would never be able to climb onto the roof. So I stood there and waited for the neighbor to stop watching.

Finally, when she went into her house, I moved as quickly as I could and ran into the church. It was a wonderful Easter.

We moved away from that area, and later I found out the police emptied out the church and shut it down completely. It made me very sad to think of that building being closed, but I know the church is more than a building, and somewhere in that city there are still Christians worshiping God together.

LIVE | DEAD CHALLENGE

In Acts 25, 26, 27, and 28, you get the feeling that something big was about to happen. Paul was gaining the attention of more officials, the Jewish population was becoming more and more angry over his preaching, and the disciples were spreading throughout the world. It was much like the days before Christ's crucifixion, and you can't help wonder where it was heading.

Chapters such as these reinforce the uncertainty of life. Nothing is guaranteed. Your life, my life—they could end at any moment. We can only pray that our years here on earth will be effective and fruitful, not to gain any success or recognition for ourselves, but to gain glory for God who has called us.

The same could be said of today's story about Esther's church—how uncertain! One day believers gathered there to worship God, and the next day the Iranian police closed it down. Neighbors she once knew and loved began to grow suspicious.

In recent months, the government has closed many of the above-ground churches in Iran. Pray that these closures will not result in the death of faith but in the scattering of seed that will bring a new harvest.

List the things you hope for right now. Are they eternal things, or are they temporal, uncertain things that you could lose at any moment? Until our entire hope is in Christ, we are destined for disappointment, uncertainty, and sadness. Reiterate your trust in Jesus, and ask where He is leading you.

...mother
...days ...
...I am
...erty. I ...
... me i...
Allah. I have a degree but ...
have children one day. Many ...
know seems joyful. What will ...
about praying to Jesus. What will become of m...
my country is beautiful. I live in fear. Ov...
I do. Heroin addiction is common. The love ...
A number of my friends have AIDS. I ...
fascinated by
the cross

Kaveh

THE TANKER

---

*The soldiers planned to kill the prisoners to prevent any of them
from swimming away and escaping. But the centurion wanted to
spare Paul's life and kept them from carrying out their plan. He
ordered those who could swim to jump overboard first and get to
land. The rest were to get there on planks or on other pieces of the
ship. In this way everyone reached land safely.*

ACTS 27:42–44

Everyone in my family knew me as someone who was angry
and bitter about life. I had been through many hardships,
and even though I practiced Islam, religion normally upset me
and made me even angrier, although I'm not sure why. Then I
became a Christian, and everything about my life changed. I felt
peace for the first time. I felt hope and happiness. Still, I didn't
tell anyone in my family that I had decided to follow Jesus.

My nephew often came to visit, and one day he asked me a
question I wasn't sure how to answer.

"What happened to you?" he asked. "Everything is different about you. The way you speak, your tone of voice, everything is different."

I tried to brush him off, but he had spent time traveling outside Iran and knew Christians from other parts of the world.

"You speak like my Christian friends in Europe. Is that what it is? Did you become a Christian as well?"

I sighed. Then I spoke.

"I did," I said. "I have become a Christian. I am a Christian."

As time went on, my nephew also converted and became a believer. But he owned a business in Iran, and because of some things that happened in his business he needed to leave Iran. The only way for him to leave was to be smuggled out. His smugglers placed him in an empty gasoline tanker, and he managed to make his way to Italy. He lived there for two years.

He had a wife and two children, and they moved in with me and my family. I taught them about Jesus and how to pray, and they became believers as well. But two years is a long time to be away from your husband, and eventually my nephew's wife decided she would do anything to get her family out of Iran.

"I'm done!" she said. "I'm finished waiting for visas and passports. I will get a tanker as my husband did, take the children inside with me, and we will get out of this country."

"I don't think that's a good idea," I said quietly. "What if you get caught? Then they'll never let you leave, and you'll probably go to prison. Just wait, be patient. Your time will come."

It even got to the point where the tanker showed up at the appointed location.

"Don't do it," I insisted. "If you really believe that Jesus can help you and be there for you, then He will make a way. Don't do this!"

She agreed to wait.

Eventually, God made a way for her. She ended up leaving the country like a queen, her bags packed, her visas stamped and ready. Everything was taken care of. She went to France, and her husband met her there. I'm so honored that God used me in those days to bring her to Christ.

LIVE | DEAD CHALLENGE

In Acts 27, the centurion used his authority to save Paul's life. It would have been easy for the centurion to remain silent, but he spoke up, and in doing this he affected the destiny of the Christian world. What if Paul had died before going to Rome? Thanks to this centurion, that didn't happen.

The same can be said of Kaveh in today's story—it would have been easier, safer perhaps, if he had not shared his faith with his nephew. But he did, and this influenced at least two generations for Christ.

How are you using your influence? Do you remain silent, or do you speak wisdom and life into the lives of others?

List three people who look to you as an influencer. How have you encouraged them lately? Have your words brought them life? Consider introducing them to the Live Dead ideals. Discuss how each of you can decide daily to die to your selfish will and live for Christ.

Search the Internet for information about Iran and pray about the news items you find. Visit the Mohabat News website and read about Christians currently in prison. Seek out information on those currently serving the Iranian people, and pray that God would lead you into a deeper level of involvement.

Determine that together you will pray and work to reach Iran with the gospel.

I have
one brother.
sick. I spe... the
cousins. I... in a
...ushed by Islam... in
I long for hope. Who can I talk to?
...into paradise? I can never please
...degree but no job. I would like to marry and
...Many of my peers use drugs to escape. hopelessness. I read
...one day. What will happen to me if I change religions? Sometin...
...joyful. What will become of my family? I am afraid. I feel sad.
...ldren ...will become of my family? I live in fear. On the Internet I see othe...
...tion is common. The love of Jesus...
...I... of my friends have A...
...by the C...

DAY TWENTY-EIGHT

Isabel

THE MOVE FROM DEATH TO LIFE

---

*For two whole years Paul stayed there in his own rented
house and welcomed all who came to see him. He proclaimed
the kingdom of God and taught about the Lord Jesus
Christ—with all boldness and without hindrance!*

ACTS 28:30–31

My childhood in Iran is cloaked in shadows and misery. The
pain I experienced when I was little turned my insides to ash.
I became a very angry young person, and when the anger would
occasionally fade it was replaced by depression and sadness.

I moved to the United States when I was in my last year
of high school. This was many, many years ago. After I finished
high school, I attended a Catholic college for a few years, but
Christianity didn't mean anything to me. Not then. But when I
look back now it seems like there was a small spark hidden inside
of me, something that yearned for God, because sometimes
late at night, when no one was in the chapel, I would go in and

pray. I would sit in the back, in the shadows, and I would look for God.

I moved to California and earned my graduate degree. I became obsessed with knowledge, obsessed with finding truth. In the middle of this obsession, I met a man and fell in love with him. We were married, and I hoped that having him in my life would make up for all the terrible pain I had experienced as a child. I guess for a short time it did, but then our relationship fell apart, and we divorced.

Up to that time, my anger had been a random force, but after the divorce my anger finally found a target: God. I remember telling someone that all the hurt in my life had turned to rage, and I was mostly mad that God would let all of these terrible things happen to me. I began to ask difficult questions.

Why did God allow these things to happen?

If life is all about pain, why am I living?

What is my purpose?

One thing kept me from killing myself: I wanted to find God, and I wanted to confront Him with my grievances. I decided that I would do everything in my power to find God, even if it meant going to the ends of the earth.

That was when I started searching for God. I went anywhere and everywhere, so long as people there were talking about God. If I heard there were New Age meetings on the other side of town, I went there. If I heard there was a large group of Hindu people somewhere, then I would go there and ask them about God. If I came across a Buddhist temple, I would go inside. I tried every religion under the sun . . . every philosophy. You name it, I tried it.

One day I even went out and bought a Koran.

Perhaps if I practice the religion of my youth, I reasoned, *God won't be angry with me anymore. Maybe Islam is the true source of all knowledge having to do with God.*

But the more I read of the Koran, the more I thought, *this is not the God I want! He is not it!*

God brought a few Christians into my life, and they invited me to church. Of course I went! But they were rather pushy—they didn't let me simply attend the services and learn more. Every week they pressed me to make a statement of faith. Every week they pressured me to get baptized. Eventually I stopped going.

It felt like I had exhausted all options. I had searched every religion and philosophy under the sun, and none had held up under my scrutiny. None had given me a direct channel to God. I was ready to end my life.

Then someone came to mind. I had attended a class with a girl named Sheryl, a Christian, and she had always talked to me about the things she read in her Bible. I remembered how one morning she had come to me and said, "Isabel, I know you have a lot of pain. I want you to know that I'm praying for you."

She had given me a book and inside the book she wrote "I know the Lord has called you."

When she gave me the book, I had thought, *yeah, whatever.* But that night, as I stared at the end of my own life, I remembered her and called her.

"Sheryl," I said, crying. "I just want to end my life. I feel so lost."

She read a few scriptures to me, and after we talked for a little while she asked me a question.

"Isabel, can you give me two days? Just two days. Come to my house for two days and after that you can do whatever you want."

So I packed a small bag and went to her house, intending to stay for the weekend.

I stayed for an entire year, and soon after that I became a Christian because I knew that Jesus was the answer to my search for God.

LIVE | DEAD CHALLENGE

When I spoke with Isabel, she was convinced that without the intervention of her friend Sheryl, she would have taken her own life. Without the love of Sheryl for her Iranian friend, and without her willingness to take her into her own home and show her the love of Christ, this story would have ended differently.

How will we respond to our Iranian friends?

Will we invite them into our lives, or will we ignore them?

The end of the book of Acts doesn't make for an excellent conclusion. We don't find out at that point what will happen to Paul or the remaining disciples. We don't know what will happen to him now that he has arrived in Rome. We're left with many loose ends.

But that's okay, because the end of the book of Acts isn't the end. It is only the beginning.

Will you join Paul?

Will you join in this quest to spread the gospel, even to the harsh regimes of the world?

Will you join Paul in declaring the word of God boldly?

Spend some time considering these questions in prayer, and then journal your response. Lay down your career or retirement plans. Consider what it would look like for you to serve the Iranian people who need to see how a Christian lives, to see how a Christian dies . . . to see how a Christian can live dead.

It's Harvest Time

BY RAYMOND OLIVER

M ost books are written to inform or entertain. This book was
written to introduce you to a group of people who are made
in the image of God, created for His praise and purpose, just as
you and I. It was written in the hope that when you hear their
stories you will love the Iranian people and pray for them, all
seventy-nine million of them!

These stories are not exceptions. They accurately represent
the longings and spiritual hunger of the Iranian people. Our
exposure to the media may lead us to believe that the people of
Iran are our enemies, but the voices of our Iranian brothers and
sisters and the voice of our Lord tell a different story.

King Cyrus, the Persian (Iranian) monarch was God's
instrument of salvation to the Jewish captives of the Old
Testament. The wise men, emissaries of the Persian royal court,
were among the first to worship Jesus. People from Iran were
present when God poured out the Holy Spirit in the book of
Acts, and the first Christian missionaries to China were Iranian.
Recently, a noted Islamic academic in Iran stated that had it not

been for the Arab invasion of AD 633, Iran would be a Christian nation today.

Nowhere are more Muslims turning to Christ than in Iran. Iranian evangelists tell us that after they have fasted and prayed, they go out to share the gospel. Between six and seven of every ten people who hear them tell the gospel will say yes to Jesus.

A spiritual harvest doesn't come on our timetable. We may choose when to plant and how much seed to sow—but only God determines if and when there will be a harvest. Our only choice in the matter is how we will respond. Harvest time comes and the clock begins ticking. You see, the time to harvest never lasts forever, and winter follows inexorably on the heels of fall. During harvest, only one thing matters—the harvest.

No delay in action is excusable.

It's harvest time! Other occupations must be deferred, lesser priorities laid aside. It is harvest time, and the harvest will not yield to our convenience, nor will it schedule its abundance around our activities. It remains in the field, an unrealized potential until it is harvested! If it is ignored, the harvest passes, never to be gathered . . . only a regret. A harvest that is not gathered is no harvest at all. A harvest gathered brings honor to the farmer and validates all the preparation and work that precedes the harvest. There is no waste so regrettable as a neglected harvest, and no joy so full as a harvest completed.

God has called us to join Him in a harvest that we did not plant. Our blood has not soaked into the Iranian soil preparing it for this day of unprecedented harvest, but the blood of many of our precious Iranian brothers and sisters in Christ has. We follow in their footsteps and gather souls in answer to their toil and suffering.

Often books such as this are written in the hopes that the information will engender intercession and support. Both of these are valid and needed responses. We however, are asking for something more. We want your voice! While we are truly grateful for your prayers on our behalf, we are looking for people who will inform and invite others into intercession, who will consider coming to serve with us, and will speak to others about the possibility of doing so as well.

We ask you to steward the information and burden this book has given you by including your network of relationships in the mission to reach Iran. Pass the book around. Start a prayer meeting on behalf of Iran. Use social media to call people to Christ's love for the people of Iran.

The people of Iran need your voice. Will you give it to them? Will you live dead?

ABOUT THE AUTHOR

S hawn Smucker is an author, blogger, and speaker who is passionate about storytelling and the importance of living an adventurous life. His recent book *Dying Out Loud: The Story of a Silk Road Nomad* tells the story of a missionary who offered everything, including his life, in order to take the message of the gospel to the unreached people in Turkey.

Shawn is a regular contributor at Deeper Church and numerous other blogs and online publications. He received his English degree from Messiah College and currently lives in Lancaster, Pennsylvania, with his wife and four children. He specializes in helping people tell their stories. You can find him on Twitter, Facebook, and at shawnsmucker.com.

Live Dead the Journey

The Live Dead Journal

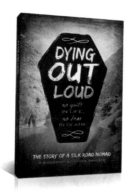

Dying Out Loud by Shawn Smucker

**For more information about these resources,
visit www.influenceresources.com.**